Retire Early and Rich

Your Own Money
Can Make You Retire Early

Rohit Gupta

Retire Early and Rich

1st Edition

MRP Rs. 299/-

ISBN: 978-93-94808-39-3

Published & Distributed by

Delta Publication

Dedication

This book is dedicated to

- My late father who always wanted me to excel in my life.
- My mother and My wife –Without their personal life sacrifices and support I could not have written this book.
- My Little daughter – whose birth inspired me to do something out of the box.
- To all my readers who will get a pathway to their dream life.

Acknowledgment

I would like to acknowledge the following people for their dedicated support and encouragement which provided me with the great courage to write this book :

- My mentor (Anup Nishane) – Who has changed my perspective on life. He has shown me the possibilities in life.
- My mentor (Dr. Sandeep Gupta) – Who encouraged me to write a book.
- My mentor (Ankit Neerav) – Who made me learn & belive in law of attraction.
- My book writing mentor (KP) – Who has provided a systematic and structured way to write the book.
- Mr. Datta Tule – Who shared his inspirational journey to financial freedom.
- My Editor (S. Lahiri and Nupur Dhingra) –Who helped by editing this book to a beautiful copy.
- My brother-in-law (Mayank Agrawal), My friend (Saransh Patidar) – They shared with me how they are confident on some assets and how they plan their investments.
- Thanks to all people who have directly or indirectly contributed to the creation of this book.
- My apologies to the people, whom I might have inadvertently missed out but they definitely are part of this exceptional journey.

I am really grateful to all people in my life who have shared their experiences with me and touched my life in any way.

To all my teachers, gurus, mentors, and friends who inspired me to write this book.

About the Book

One thing that comes to everyone is old age. Retirement is always connected with old age and it's the most ignored aspect of everyone's life. We don't have any clue how to plan it effectively at our younger ages. And Sometimes people take so much time to think about retirement, that they don't have much time to plan it effectively. This book is an initiative to give the correct guidance at the correct time to the people with the money they already have in their life.

About the Author

Coming from a service-class family, getting educated and start earning was the main motto of his life. He is a management graduate in finance, currently pursuing Charted Wealth Manager. In the last 13 years, after working with fortune 50 companies of the world, he got a chance to understand the personal financial issues faced by people which he has tried to resolve by the help of this book. His mission is to help more than 1,000,000 people across India to understand the importance of planning retirement early in life.

CONTENTS

Prelude

The world is changing and evolving so rapidly. It is not a revolution in the traditional sense, but the organisational transformation has grown so widespread on a worldwide scale. The reasons could be numerous; economic recession, AI growth, cost reduction, and improved operational efficiency.

Anand had migrated to Mumbai from his hometown in Bihar decades ago. He considered himself lucky to get a job almost immediately unlike his other friends who had migrated with him. Anand, like his other friends, was a graduate and was getting accustomed to the big city with all its idiosyncracies. Anand worked in a reputed company and so had to maintain a lifestyle that suited his social status. He started shopping in the malls, eating out, having parties, and using unwanted avenues for expenditure like credit cards. He had also accumulated a lot of items like furniture, gadgets, and articles of clothing which he could well do without. Soon he ascended the corporate ladder to assume a position of eminence and accepted the demands of his parents and elders to marry and have children. His social compulsions had prompted him to buy a rather lavish house, car and put his children into expensive schools. A major portion of his salary went into EMIs and other social obligations. Time and again he put off thoughts of the future in order to manage the present. However, time and tide wait for no man and in 2020, the deadly COVID-19 pandemic struck the world. Not many entities or establishments could bear the stigma brought in by the marauding virus. Anand and his family got infected and so did his parents in their hometown. To make matters worse, Anand's company decided to downsize looking at the declining business. Anand's hospital bills had skyrocketed and he rued not having a proper Mediclaim to help him out. His company had retrenched him and thus it was difficult for him to pay the EMIs and the credit card bills.

Soon, he started selling his car and other amenities to keep up with the expenses.

Warren Buffet once said, "If you buy things that you do not need, soon you will have to sell things you need." Anand had come across this quote several times but had always put off his worries for another day. However, the day of reckoning hit him harder than expected. He was left penniless, jobless, helpless, and most pathetically... hopeless.

A lot of Anands have been jolted by the ravages of time because of their unplanned, disorganized, and disoriented ways of living. Money is a strange commodity. It requires utmost care and proper management. There are many tools and media to keep one updated on the latest facilities available to make money work for an individual to the optimum level. However, in the rush for a daily living often people like Anand procrastinate such important planning for a later date. Sometimes, that later date never arrives or when it does the damage has already been done.

It is important to plan one's financial future in advance and with proper care. The utility of this book makes it more prominent due to the sheer uncertainty of the times. While it is important to alleviate the status of such Anands of urban India should also be cared for.

It is not a difficult task. Just awareness is all that matters.

- Do you want to enjoy your life with energy, time, and money?
- Do you want to retire early in life to enjoy your dreams before you get too old?
- Do you want to break away from the crowd and be different than just a "brick in the wall"?
- Do you want to understand the rapid changes that are happening in the financial sphere?
- Do you want to keep yourself updated with the new norms that taking over the market?
- Are you sure that your work/job will get you to attain the goals of your life?
- How long can you go without a consistent income if you lost your work today?
- How long can you support your family and satisfy your obligations?
- Don't you think financial preparation could save you from the disasters coming your way?
- Do you often rue about missed chances?
- Do you fear that your hard work would not provide "you" with the fruit that it should?
- Are you conservative and unwilling to take risks?
- Do you want to know about wise investments?

The world has changed rapidly over the past few years. The age-old suggestions on having a good life have become obsolete and have been replaced by new methods. The

"New Normal" has ushered in the importance of smart work over mere hard work and the pandemic has also thrown up glaring lessons to be learnt.

It is important to break-away from age-old myths and get into the "growth mentality" stature rather than sticking to the "survival mode" status. There are proven ways to get there. I am committed to hand hold people who are action-takers and who want to have a better life to enjoy "NOW"!

It is easy to walk along the beaten tracks but that does not necessarily guarantee you accomplishments of the life that you might yearn for.

An age-old adage says: "Flow with the times, or be influential enough to change the times."

I say it in a different way: "Those who seek, explore, learn and act diligently always blossom amongst thorns."

TRY IT!!

"Life throws countless burdens on people, not to make them feeble but to make them strong."

Chapter1: Introduction

"Personal finance is self-responsibility, accept it today or regret it later."

Every activity and its success revolve around three attributes which are; time, money, and energy. Contentment or a sense of achievement and joy comes upon us only when these three aspects of life are utilized to the optimum proportion.

From our early 20s to our 30s we experience the most youthful stage of our life. Generally, at this period we do have great reserves of time and energy, but little money to supplement the attainment of our wishes. This is the time to learn, explore and discover. In this age, wealth only means money to us.

During the age of early 40s to late 50s, we tend to reach the zenith of our careers. This is the time when people make money, have reasonably good savings, and create an economically stable ecosystem. However, during this period there might be reserves of money and energy available but little time to make use of the same. Here wealth means Time to us.

After we attain the age of 60 and beyond, though we might have enough reserves of money and time, we are left with little or no energy to be able to enjoy the other resources. Here wealth means health to us.

Thus, in life, we are always left with one of the core components to ensure the full enjoyment of our life. Life will have a different joy, if we can have all the 3 components of time , money and energy together.

Often we might come across someone in our family - maybe an elderly relative who might have worked hard throughout his life and is known for having a healthy bank balance but is barely able to walk. Time and again people might have heard him musing, "What am I going to do with this much money? It is my grandchildren who will enjoy it."

The plight of that relative makes us ponder time and again whether we might also end up in the same situation later in our life. Can we not come out of this age-old malaise and enjoy life at every stage of livelihood?

"Oh, the worst of all tragedies is not to die young, but to live until I am seventy-five and yet not ever truly to have lived."

– Martin Luther King Jr.

Most people today are jostled in this vicious cycle of life. When we were in school, we were told once you get good marks in 10th ,life will be good. However, after the 10th ,we were told once you get good marks in 12th ,life will become graceful. During the last phase of college or even before that, we are advised to work hard to get proper placements so that life becomes gracious. After we get a job, it becomes imminent to work hard during the initial 5 years of the job to get settled with the new environment. Once we gain 5 years of experience and acquire reasonably good knowledge in our domain, we are prompted to switch jobs to attract a better package and get married in search of the elusive balance of life. After achieving this,we are often informed to be attached to the assurance of balance in life like purchasing a house having a child, or having a good amount of savings, we still remain entwined within priorities and responsibilities. During our 40s & 50s, we keep working harder, as per the social parameters to attract bigger packages to finish off our loans and other impediments to be able to unburden ourselves. At 50 and beyond and we are grappled with the apprehensions and duty toward children's education, marriage, and least priority is given to our own retirement. Once this is done, it appears that life would be peaceful as never before. People like us keep working hard day and night in the quest for a better future for themselves and their families. However, when they retire, they don't have the energy to enjoy life to the utmost. A vast majority of the middle-class, working population falls within this torturous bracket of life. Many people are unable to reach even retirement age. The credit for this, of course, goes to the noxiousness of the stressful lifestyle of the modern era, to quite an extent. So, we face challenges at every stage of life, be it in childhood when we learn to walk on our tiny legs or during old age after gaining the utmost experience, social status, and hefty wealth. We need to strike a balance between our responsibilities and our happiness and should take the time to live this beautiful life.

"A person starts dying when they stop dreaming."

-- Brian Williams

We have all fostered many dreams and goals since our formative years. However, the mercilessness of time has often made us compromise with them. Haven't we all gone past attractive shops and restaurants and suppressed our wishes for another day? Haven't we, sometimes or the other seen our dream car or villa on TV, in a magazine and cursed our luck or wondered - will I be able to buy this ever? Haven't we been rattled and jealous by seeing our friends, relatives, or associates going to various exotic destinations and wondered why had God not given us such opportunities? Have you ever wondered why only a handful of the population achieve their dreams while others keep languishing in misery? **It is true that most people just survive while only a handful is able to live.** Yes, you read that correctly, most people just survive for the next moment as long as there is breath in the body. Why only some people with no background or pedigree are able to reach lofty heights which no one from their generation had been able to reach? This is all because most of them had a plan for their lives. You might be thinking now, that some people are born rich. Leave those people in your count since they were born with a silver spoon but you might be not, so keep the focus on yourself while reading. Do not think what works for anyone else will work for you as well. If you do well in your life, it's your family and you who will be having a better life, not your neighbours, relatives, colleagues, or friends. For some time, you need to become selfish and concentrate on what you are doing for the good life that you have always yearned for. Now, you might say I already have a good life. It's good if you already have a good life, but have you ever thought about whether or not you want to keep working throughout life, get retired, and wait for the last moments of your life? Or are you someone who wants to retire early and is looking for someone who can help you with this by giving you a proper methodology? You are lucky to be reading this, you will definitely get a pathway from this book which can really help you to retire early and enjoy it. Let me explain this to you with the wonderful story of two friends.

There were two friends, Rahul and Rohit living in the city of Pune. Rahul was fresh out of college and had joined a new job recently. Rohit was a person who used to help people with wealth creation goals and methods to retire early. Though there was an age gap of 10 years between them, Rahul always used to seek advice from Rohit as he used to consider him to be his elder brother. Rahul in his childhood used to think that he will be having a lot of money when he will start earning and would live his dream life without the need of thinking about money. He had seen his friend cum brother helping many people with finances.

So, one day he went to his home and said, "Rohit *bhaiya* - I want your help. I am doing a job today as my parents wanted me to get educated and start earning so that I get a good life. However, I feel I don't want to work throughout my life as I have seen an uncle of mine who has all the money now but is just waiting for his death. At the same time, I don't want to leave the job which is giving me a salary for paying up my education loan and is helping me to meet my all other important expenses. As you help people with finances, can you help me to know what needs to be done considering my goals? How can I use my salary towards it?"

Rohit said, "Yes Rahul. I am happy to see that you have started thinking in this direction so early in your life. Most people take a lifetime to understand it. Even some people on their deathbeds agree that they did not live their life fully. I will definitely help you. But before starting on it, let me explain to you different concepts on finances."

Let us all like Rahul, get access to the pearls of wisdom, Rohit is about to share in the next chapters. Believe me! The knowledge shared hereby and the application of the methods revealed will take you nearer to your cherished dream.

Come, let's live our lives and not just survive through the times.

Chapter2: Financial Concepts

"An investment in knowledge pays the best interest."

– Benjamin Franklin

There are many modes to ensure financial security. Though some of the traditional forms of savings and building one's financial portfolio might seem obsolete, there are enough options for people to tread the right path by analyzing one's financial plans. In the same context, it is paramount to properly comprehend some of the common concepts in this domain.

Investment:

An investment is an asset, object, or systematic plan that is acquired or adopted to generate income or the appreciation of one's financial health. Investments are done in pursuit of proper planning toward future goals. Investments may be short-term, medium-term, or long-term. An investment happens in the form of expenditure of some resources like time, effort, money, or asset in the present times - in the hope of receiving greater payoffs in the future.

For Example: If someone purchases a house and gives it out on rent, the house will provide him recurring income over a period and also have an asset value for him. He may also sell the house at a much higher value in the future.

There are different investment avenues available in the market like exchange-traded funds, direct equity, indirect equities (Mutual Funds), Government Bonds, real estate, commodity trade, sale of antique items, and much more. In the present era cryptocurrencies, NFTs, etc are also making their way into the market. There are many options available for investments. However, one must choose the proper modes based on his/her investment horizon, the requirement of returns, risk appetite, safety of instrument, liquidity of money , tax efficiency and many such factors. Investments are mandatory to fulfill all future goals and to manage expenses, exigencies, or emergencies.

Income:

Income refers to the money that a person or entity receives in exchange for services rendered or the sale of products. It's the basic ingredient of investment and creates the basis to enter into its zone. The quality and consistency of your income decide the types and quantity of investments. Since investment leads to long-term corpus building, the consistency of income decides the corpus that you create from your investments. Income for most people means their total earnings in the form of wages, salaries, and returns on their investments that they receive at some defined frequency, which maybe on a daily, weekly, or monthly basis. For businesses, income means the revenues that are accrued from the rendering of services, the sale of products, or the receipt of any kind of interest/dividend, etc. Different types of characteristics of incomes differ in nature and can be broadly categorized as:

1. Active Income – It is the revenue earned against active work or real-time activity. A job or business which requires our active involvement brings about active income.
2. Passive Income – It's the income that is generated even when we are not actively involved. It is rather a process or a system that generates money for us even when we might be asleep. There are different passive income sources like blogs, YouTube videos, royalties from books & many other similar avenues.

For generating a sustainable income, we should first gather enough knowledge about the requirements of the market, about high-paid skill sets, and about our own areas of interest. A deep study is needed to grasp the concepts through which people might be getting highly-paid jobs or might be running successful business ventures. Properly planned, strategic investments can also create a lot of wealth. It can be through direct equity, real estate, and several available options. However, a regular and consistent flow of income is required to enable or empower people to invest wisely in an effort for creating wealth.

Expenses:

Expenses are the amounts that go out of your pocket in exchange for goods or services. Some expences are legitimate and inevitable but there are expenses that are mostly unnecessary. A house to live in, food, medicine, utilities like water, electricity, phone bills, cable tv, gas, newspaper, internet, etc. are indispensable expenses. Household items and clothing also come under the same bracket. Fuel and travel expenses towards work and family compulsions are necessities too. Another important expenditure happens for education which cannot be overlooked. Expenses towards entertainment, vacations, dinner outings, movies, and sports events are although not necessities but do appear to be part of the agenda of life. Many people indulge in wasteful and unnecessary expenses which gives them little scope for investments. These expenses are mostly triggered by the alluring advertisements on social and print media and other online platforms. Many people have expenses more than their income and because of this they take loans and get into debt traps. One loan compels one to go for other loans and soon a person gets engulfed in a vicious circle. Investments should be considered to be an important expense. Everyone should plan to invest the money as the first priority soon after having an income flow. To have a prosperous and trouble-free life, a healthy balance between income and expenditure should be maintained. The difference between needs and desires are needed to be understood properly to track all expenses.

"Too many people spend money they earned, to buy things they don't want, to impress people they don't like."

– Will Rogers

Needs and desires:

Needs and desires are the basis of all expenses. As a human, we all have needs, demands, and luxuries to fulfill. We should be able to define our needs and desires correctly in our life from early on because if we don't have the definition of the needs and the desires clearly defined in our minds, our desires overcome our senses to transform into necessities without our realization. The basic difference between needs, demands, and luxuries in life can be explained with an example.

There are 3 people – Ram, Ramesh, and Laxman. All of them feel hungry at the same time.

Ram eats home made food to fulfil his basic need of hunger.

Ramesh wants to eat a burger to fulfil his hunger. Ramesh's need is now more of a demand in response to his hunger.

Laxman wants to eat at KFC, MC Donald's, or some exotic outlet to fulfil his basic need of hunger. This is a classic example of luxury.

We all should understand clearly what the needs in our lives are and what the demands in our lives are. If we do not control our demands or luxuries properly, then demands and luxuries take no time to become part of our life resulting in unnecessary expenses. A commonly used formula can be used to bifurcate needs, demands-luxuries, and savings, investments. The formula is 50:30:20. From the income that we earn every month, 50% of it should go towards necessities. It may be rent, Utility bills, Groceries, House or car EMI, Insurance expenses, and many such things that cannot be avoided. 30% should go towards demands and luxuries. It may be dining out, shopping, travel, and many such things that are not necessary and can be avoided by looking for better alternatives. The remaining 20% should go towards savings and investments which will help you reach nearer to short-term and long-term financial goals. We can think of swapping the demand & luxury proportion with savings to have a better outcome. future. This 50:30:20 will be beneficial when you have started working. Later with increase of income, our focus should be to increase the investments. More amount goes towards investments , sooner you will be able to create a a better corpus for a comfortable and desirable future

Investment instruments:

Investment avenues are different methods and modes of investment. Knowing about different investment avenues is very important so that we can choose the best options to realise our goals in our life. Different investment instruments have their own benefits and disadvantages. Before going for any investment, we need to think about the factors below:

- Do we understand each component of the investment we want to take up?

- Do we understand the risk appetite?

- Do we have the required investment horizon?

- Will we be able to continue the investment for the period it demands?

- Does the Investment instrument really provide the returns you really require or it is just imaginary returns?

- How safe is the investment instrument?

- How tax efficient is the investment instrument?

For Example: There are 2 people Ram and Shyam. Ram's daughter is about to go for graduation 2 years from now.

So, his priority should be capital protection and should be away from any instrument that invests in equities. Similarly, Shyam's daughter would be going for her graduation after 5 years from now. So, he can think of investing in equities as he has sufficient time to invest and get capital appreciation.

Everyone needs to have a check on risk appetite, rate of returns, liquidity, lock-in, tax implications, and the year of the target (goal) before committing to any investment. Understanding an investment instrument is recommended for getting the best benefits from the same. You can take help from experts if needed, but don't take the advice of any novice who is also sailing in the same boat as you. They might not be able to give you correct advice as they are unaware of the right options.

In Chapter3, 4 we have dedicated information for understanding commonly used investment instruments.

Inflation:

Inflation is the regular increase in prices of goods and services and the subsequent devaluation of the currency. It makes the money in your hand have diminishing value as time passes due to the increase in prices. Inflation leads to higher prices and lower purchasing power. It is impacting the life of every human being whether they understand it or not. Blaming the government or any statutory organization for inflation is wrong since it is a trend that has carried through history and will always remain.

For Example: Petrol was Rs.20/Litre in 1995 and in 2022 it reached near to 120. To have a better life in the future, you need to plan your investments in a way to beat inflation. If you are not planning your life by taking inflation into account, then you are preparing for your own doom, as the cost of things will keep rising with each coming year.

Chapter 5 is an in-depth elaboration on inflation for better understanding.

Investment Analysis:

Investment analysis is a way to analyze investments already done in the past. When we had committed to investment, we had some goals in our minds. Our goals however might change with the changing times as :

-- Your responsibilities are different being single, married, divorced , parents.

-- Your children are going to school / College or now are in a job or getting married.

-- Your goals and dreams have changed with time.

-- You might want to retire early or start a new business.

So , with the changing times we need to check time and again whether the investments are in line with the goals that we are targeting. This is the biggest miss in most of the people's investments.

All the big companies release their quarterly statements to check if they are in the right direction as per their goals and targets. Similarly, we as individuals should also do our own analysis on a monthly basis. If not possible on monthly basis, at least this should be done on a quarterly, half-yearly, or yearly basis. With changing times, there are a lot of new investment avenues coming up and even our goals keep changing with time. So, analyzing our investments will help us to alter the investment instrument if needed within the required timeframe. We should really be thoughtful as we are investing our hard-earned money. Knowing whether our money is flowing in the right direction and would yield the required returns or not, is important for our successful financial future. Not analyzing the investments means we are just relying on luck without doing much ourselves.

Chapter 6 has been dedicated to investment analysis for better understanding.

Financial Plan:

A financial plan is a roadmap toward all future goals. For a stable and pleasant future, we should have a strong financial plan. It is just like having a smooth road trip along a super expressway. We mark the important points or milestones on a map before we start traveling. Similarly, in a financial plan, we mark the financial goals and the proposed time for their realization. It is the first step towards the fulfilment of one's future financial goals. It acts as a bridge between one's current reality and all the financial goals one may foster in mind. It is the step-by-step approach towards reaching every goal. It keeps proper track of investments, expenses, income, needs, and desires in life. It helps us to save money so that we may easily achieve our ultimate goal. It becomes a guaranteed solution if you start early and be disciplined. Whatever we might yearn to achieve, can only be accomplished if we can link our dreams and our current life with a properly defined financial plan.

People fear hearing the word financial plan. Though it may sound complicated, however, it is actually, very simple. It's neither rocket science nor a difficult question of maths. You just need to walk on the defined path with discipline. It is just a way forward in the pursuit of happiness.

"It is very simple to be happy, but it is very difficult to be simple."

– Rabindranath Tagore

A personal financial plan typically includes the following baseline data:

- Personal information e.g. Age, income, children, residential status, etc.
- Financial goals that are important (Child Education, Child marriage, Retirement planning) and dreams (dream house, dream car, dream vacation)
- An overview of the big picture (assets, debt, etc.).
- Different types of incomes, expenses and recurring investments
- Different insurance covers either mandatory or optional

Based on the above details, a finance professional can help by charting out a debt elimination plan, an investment plan to build assets, the best-optimized way to reach financial dreams/goals, and income tax strategies for better tax planning. One should definitely have a financial plan, for getting certainty in your life.

"The biggest risk of all is not taking one."

– Mellody Hobson

Risk Analysis:

Risk analysis is analyzing risks and taking decisions accordingly. It is very important for everyone because different people in different age groups have different needs and risk appetites. Needs and risk-appetites serve as the prime attributes for deciding on an investment instrument. It helps people to check if the future goals are in sync with the current risk taken in the investment instrument.

This should be done with utmost care as one small mistake may ensnare one into the wrong potholes of misguided investment instruments leading to substandard returns.

For Example: A person aged 59, who is on the verge of retirement has 80% of investment in equity. This means the risk analysis is wrongly done and needs to be rectified with immediate effect.

Rohit – "Rahul, Now you might have got a good understanding of financial concepts that are important for your personal finances."

Rahul – "Yes *bhaiyya*. Can you now tell me, how I can invest strategically to build a sizeable corpus?"

Rohit – "Yes Rahul, let me first tell you what are the important things to do before committing to investments."

Chapter3: Planning

"There are dreamers and there are planners; the planners make their dreams come true."

– Edwin Louis Cole

Why Planning

Planning is essential to stay focused on goals despite the constant development of situations around us. We all have hopes, dreams, and aspirations in life. However, how many of us actually go on to achieve our goals? Often, we spend a lot of time thinking or talking about what we want but do not take the proper steps to achieve it. It's not because we're lazy. It's because we don't know from where to start and how to start since we don't have a plan. Planning the life we want, can serve as a roadmap or guide to make those dreams a reality.

It can help during the following:

- Whenever it appears that life is spiralling out of control.
- There is a struggle to make decisions.
- We feel that we are lost and lack direction.

It is the process of deciding in detail how to do something before we actually start doing it.

Think about this for a second:

- Whenever we travel, we plan our trip.
- Before getting married, one always plans for the wedding.
- Before throwing a party, one plans the event.
- If we want to make more money, we need to plan for it.

In all the above cases every activity was assisted by a plan and the better the plan, the greater the chances of success in the execution of the same. Every form of greatness that we see around us has a much deeper foundation. Similarly, planning things way ahead of time helps us to have a smooth financial journey that is not punctuated by emergencies and mishaps. Proper planning is the most important aspect before committing to any financial proposition as it helps to access all aspects properly from every possible angle, way ahead of time before the execution.

Emergency Fund:

An emergency fund is a spare cash that is used during financial distress and emergencies. People who had managed to keep some reserves of the emergency fund were able to survive and sustain through the Covid-19 pandemic.

The primary purpose of the fund is to meet emergency expenses during unforeseen circumstances. Emergencies can be of any form ranging from short-term requirements to long-term exigencies.

Short-term emergencies can be unexpected like repair works at home, breakdown of any item at home/car, unexpected family travels, theft or burglary at home or during a journey, uninsured illness needing costly medicines and treatment.

Long-term emergencies can be prolonged duration of job loss, medical or family conditions requiring a long break from work, damage to a house in a natural calamity, a long break after maternity, or uninsured chronic illness requiring a big amount.

It should be calculated based on the current monthly expenses. Here all expenses should be thought of as one may encounter them throughout the year as well. It can be cumulative of one's 3-12 months of current monthly expenses. The primary objective of this fund is to help people when they need it urgently and without any delay. While some emergencies may give the space of a few hours or days to prepare, others may require funds immediately. Therefore, the avenues that one should use to park their emergency fund should be highly liquid and easily accessible. People can keep these amounts in auto-sweep fixed deposits, liquid mutual funds, or even use the over-draft facilities of loan products. The overdraft facility of the loan products can help in saving a reasonably good amount on interest as well. Most people today have a home loan and they do prepayment when they have funds available. Instead of doing pre-payment, one can keep those amounts in an over-draft account to save on interest and utilize that amount in case of emergencies if needed. People should plan for an emergency fund properly as it saves them from breaking other investments or taking extra loans to fulfil their needs during emergencies.

"Planning is thinking about the future and doing something about it now."

Term Insurance:

Term insurance is a life insurance plan, which provides high life cover at affordable rates. Life is unpredictable, we can plan for our future but we can never assure whatever we have planned would get to taste the fruits of success. You may not always be around to take care of your family and that's when a term plan ensures your family is well protected. It provides financial coverage to the policyholder's family against a fixed amount of premium for a specified period of time which is denoted by the policy term. If the insured individual dies when the policy is active, a death benefit is paid to the nominees of the insured individual. Term insurance not only provides financial protection to the family in cases of most unfortunate events, but it also has various other benefits as well:

- Multiple Death Benefit Pay-out Options.
- Additional riders for different needs.
- Income Tax Benefits.
- Critical illness coverage.
- Accidental death benefit coverage.

Proper planning for opting for the right type of insurance should be the first priority of any individual before going for the investment.

For Example: Ram and Shyam both work in the same company, ABC, and are of the same age. One day while working in the office Shyam suffered a heart attack and passed away. Shyam's family had to suffer a lot as Shyam had a home loan, a small daughter, and a wife who is a homemaker (housewife) and he was the only breadwinner of the house. After his demise, his wife had to sell their house and complete the due amount for the loan, and kept the remaining amount in the bank account for her daughter's education and other needs. If Shyam would have taken a term insurance policy, his family could have lived in their own house without getting bothered by the obstacles in the future. This incident provided Ram with a lesson and he immediately bought a term cover for himself. Nobody wants to become a Shyam for his family. One mistake of his has landed his family in deep trouble.

For deciding the term insurance amount, important factors to consider are insurance premium, claim settlement ratio, features like death benefit, critical illness covered, waiver of premium, and various such riders. Another important thing to check which is ignored by most people is to make a list of loans and liabilities that one may currently be carrying, current monthly expenses, number of dependent people like parents, children, or a homemaker (wife) currently depending on the income. This will help to have adequate coverage insurance amount. Everyone should plan to take term insurance when they are young as when one starts aging the premium keeps increasing with each passing birthday.

For Example: Ramesh and Pankaj are two friends, aged 25 years, working in the same company. They attended a session at their company regarding term insurance and Ramesh got convinced to buy term insurance. However, Pankaj remained adamant and refused to invest citing it to be a waste of money. Ramesh bought term insurance by paying approximately Rs. 13000/per annum for one-crore cover, till he turned 60 years of age. This premium of Rs. 13000 would be the same till he turned 60. Now Pankaj, after 7 years understood the importance and thought of buying term insurance. He was required to pay around Rs. 20000 for the same one crore insurance. Now, this increased premium of Pankaj will remain the same for the remaining years. **Ramesh will be paying 4,55,000 during the whole tenure and Shyam will be paying 5,60,000. Here Shyam has not saved money. Instead he paid 1,05,000 extra by delaying the decision and during this tenure of 7 years, his family was at complete risk.**

One mistake is commonly done by people and that becomes the prime reason for their claim rejection. Mistake is they provide false information about pre-existing diseases, smoker/non-smoker category or any other information. Insurance companies directly reject the claim, when they come to know that false information was provided while taking this policy. Most people do this, to save on premiums now. What people do not realize is that this term insurance was taken for the benefit of their family when they will not be with them. I am sure no one wants their family members to run away from pillar to post for getting this claim and finally getting rejected.

If we don't have term insurance and something happens to the earning member of the family then the complete family has to suffer. I am sure nobody wants the family members to face a miserable condition where they have to ask friends and relatives for monetary help. One should understand the fact that this is an investment for the betterment of the future of your loved ones, not a wastage.

Health Insurance:

A health insurance policy is a product that protects a person against the financial implications of a wide variety of health-related expenses, ranging from those caused by minor illnesses and injuries to critical diseases. Therefore, health insurance serves as a protective financial shield for people in case of a major medical expense. It reimburses the bills or pays the medical care provider directly on behalf of the individual. Comprehensive medical insurance cover the cost of hospitalization, day-care procedural expenses, medical care at home (domiciliary hospitalization), and ambulance charges, amongst others.

A health insurance plan helps people to stay covered against various diseases. Additionally, it helps to boost tax savings too. Under section 80D of the Income Tax Act, 1961, one can claim tax benefits against one's health insurance premium.

Benefits of buying health insurance:

1. Health Check-ups every year.
2. Covers Out-Patient-Duty requirements.
3. Covers pre and post-hospitalization.
4. Covers pre-existing diseases.
5. Provides cashless treatments.
6. Provides additional sum insured.
7. Provides tax benefits.

People should think of buying health insurance earlier in life as the chances of having a disease in old age are higher as compared to when one is young. In case you get some disease and you think of buying health insurance, then either you will not get a favourable policy, or even if you get one, it will be at a much higher price. Along with term insurance, this should be mandatorily availed by everyone, otherwise, the cost of negligence might be too high.

For Example: There was a person called Rakesh who was quite a reckless person. He did not have any health insurance, as he thought that since he was fit and fine why should he waste money on health insurance premiums? He recently changed his job and was coming back from office celebrating his last day in his company. On the way, he met with a major accident and he got admitted to the hospital. He had to pay Rs.1 lakh for the complete treatment out of his pocket as he did not have the corporate cover because of leaving the job. His family did not have that amount, so they took a personal loan to pay this amount. This loan has added an extra EMI which could have been avoided in case he had medical insurance.

If Rakesh had separate health insurance other than corporate, he could have saved Rs. 1 lakh he had to pay for his treatment and could have avoided the hassles of having a personal loan as well.

There are various aspects to check before buying health insurance: whether the premium is on the lower side, claim settlement is good, hospitals covered are nearby, no sub-limits on room caping or on specific diseases and other policy features should be as per our need. There are so many domiciliary benefits that are provided by insurance companies with add-on riders that could help the sufferer with the treatment at their place as well. Having proper health insurance helps us to save various costs involved in case of any health issues. This can lead us to a deep financial crisis as well. So, this should be mandatorily taken by all.

Vehicle Insurance:

It refers to ensuring one's vehicle against unfortunate and unpredictable incidents. It is a mandatory insurance cover that every vehicle owner in India must have, be it a car, truck, tractor, or two-wheeler. It safeguards against accidental damages or theft of the vehicle and also safeguards against third-party legal liability for bodily injury and/or property damage. It also provides personal accident cover for the owner-driver/occupants of the vehicle. Motor vehicle insurance can be bought through online or offline modes from companies authorized by the Insurance Regulatory and Development Authority of India (IRDAI).

Types:

1. The Third-party Vehicle Insurance Policy – It is a basic plan and is mandatory as per The Motor Vehicles Act. Not owning this basic vehicle insurance plan while driving/riding in India can lead to heavy monetary penalties. It covers the vehicle owner's liabilities in case the insured vehicle injures a third party or damages their property.
2. The Comprehensive Vehicle Insurance Policy-- It includes the benefits of a Third-party Vehicle Insurance Policy as well as covers damages to the vehicle in case of an accident, fire, riots, or man-made and natural calamities. This policy offers enhanced coverage.

3. Zero depreciation cover – It is also known as bumper to bumper cover. With zero depreciation cover insurer does not have to pay the depreciation cost in case of depreciation of the damaged or replaced parts and policy holder can claim the full amount. Typically, during claim settlement, an insurer deducts the depreciation value of parts before replacing the damaged parts. However, with this add-on, there's no such deduction, and you receive the 100% claim amount (apart from any other specified deductibles or applicable costs as per the policy's terms and conditions).

For Example: Mahesh was having comprehensive insurance for his car. While on vacation, his car met with an accident. As the insurance was comprehensive, car was not fully covered and he has to pay 20,000 from his pocket.

Although the government has made third-party insurance as mandatory but people should definitely take zero depreciation coverage to cover all the costs involved in case of an accident.

Travel Insurance

It is a unique product that offers you financial assistance in case something goes wrong while one is traveling.

Imagine being in a situation where the luggage had been misplaced, or someone has been a victim of theft in a foreign country. Dealing with such situations can be expensive and difficult. That is precisely why travel insurance is so crucial!

It covers a range of scenarios, including medical and dental emergencies, theft of money, loss of passport or other important documents, flight cancellation, and misplacement or lost luggage.

For Example: Mohan was going to visit his cousin in Europe. He has taken travel insurance unwillingly as it was mandatory to travel. After reaching Europe, he felt ill because of climatic changes. He has to get hospitalized where his insurance cover was used after paying some mandatory amount. Has he not been covered, he would have paid the entire amount by his pocket.

Many countries have mandated travel insurance to travel to their countries, but travellers should definitely take travel insurance to avoid the hassles and have a joyful journey.

"Planning saves you from big collapses of the future."

Tax planning:

Tax planning is the analysis of one's financial situation from a tax efficiency point of view to plan one's finances in the most optimized manner. It helps people to utilize tax exemptions, deductions, and benefits in the best possible way to minimize the tax burden. It is the process of analyzing a financial plan or a situation from a tax perspective. It ensures that all elements of a financial plan can function together with maximum tax efficiency. It is one of the significant components of a financial plan. Reducing tax liabilities and increasing the ability to make contributions towards retirement plans are critical for success.

There are many tax-saving options for all taxpayers as mentioned below. These options allow a wide range of exemptions and deductions that help in limiting the overall tax liability. Below mentioned are the sections:

80 C – life insurance premiums, tuition fees, housing loan principal payment, PPF, tax saving mutual funds (ELSS), ULIP, NSC, Sukanya Samridhi account, FD.

80 CCC – For amount deposited in annuity plan of LIC or any other insurer for a pension from a fund referred to in Section10(23AAB).

80 CCD(1) – Employee contribution to NPS account.

80 CCD(2) – Employer's contribution to NPS account.

80 CCD (1) (B) - New pension scheme.

80 D – Health insurance paid for self, spouse and children, parents, senior citizens, preventive health check-ups.

80 DD – Treatment of dependent and the handicapped.

80 DDB – Treatment of specified diseases for non-senior citizens and senior citizens.

80 E – Interest on education loans.

80 EEA – Additional tax benefit on affordable houses.

80 EEB – Interest on loan for the purchase of the electric vehicle.

80 G – Donations to charitable funds or institutions.

80 GGA – Donations to scientific research or rural development.

80 GGC – Donation to political parties.

80 GG – If you pay rent but don't receive HRA from the employer.

80 TTA – Interest on the savings account.

80 TTB – Interest received by senior citizens.

80 U- Physically handicapped resident – self.

10(13A)- House rent allowance.

10(14)-Children Education

10(5)- Leave travel allowances for traveling in the country.

24 -- Interest component of home loan.

Tax-saving blunders that most people often make:

- Mixing insurance and investments.
- Investment planning not done with respect to tax-saving instruments
- Investing in dependents spouse (there are better ways: Parents/ HUF/company)
- Creating auto-renewal Fixed Deposit.
- Hiding correct income from the department.
- Not filing ITR (lands you in problems when applying for loans).
- Buy without thinking that the investment can help you in wealth creation instead.
- Buying at the end of the year just to claim taxes.
- Various times companies (Employer, Insurance) pay after deducting TDS (Tax deducted at source). Sometimes it was wrongly deducted and has to be claimed while filing ITR.

For Example -- Ramesh gets 10 lakhs in inheritance. He has a loan remaining of 10 lakhs with 10 years tenure at

9%. He is confused should I repay the loan or continue the loan.

Let us see if he continues with the loan and utilizes these 10 lakhs for investment, how it will benefit him:

	Year 1-9 EMI 12668	Year 10 EMI 11612
Principal + Interest Component	152011 Every Year	139343 on the 10th year
Tax @10% Every Year	152011*10% =15201	139343*10 =13934
Tax @20% Every Year	152011*20% =30402	139343*20 =27869
Tax @30% Every Year	152011*30% =45603	139343*30 =41803

	Total Tax Saved Year 1-9	Total Tax Saved Year 10	Gross Total Tax Saved
Tax Saved @10%	15201*9 =138609	13934*1=13934	150743
Tax Saved @20%	30402*9=273618	27869*1=27869	301487

Tax Saved @30%	45603*9=410427	41803*1=41803	452230

Now you might think, we would have paid Rs 5,20,109 extra by continuing the loan. If you would have invested that 10lakhs @12%, you would have received Rs 31,05,848. This is roughly 6 times of the amount you would have paid. Here we have not considered the amounts, you would have saved in taxes every year and invested. It will also generate some returns for you. So, you might have understood if taxes are used efficiently, it can be beneficial for financial wealth.

Things to check before planning:

- One should segregate the primary income across multiple PANs. Personal PAN for salary and business income under HUF/ private limited/ partnership should be separate.

- One should anticipate the expenses for the year like rent, health insurance, life insurance, vacations, and existing EMIs, and optimize one's salary for maximum exemptions.

- One should claim deductions for things that they would anyway spend money on eg: Health insurance, term insurance, interest, and principal component of a home loan.

- One should claim deductions if they spend money to support a disabled dependent, self, or medical care.

- One should invest money based on goals and one's risk-taking ability without considering tax savings only.

- One should claim deductions for investments that are tax savings in the financial plan.

- One should check and weigh the option that is most suitable to one's portfolio – old and new tax regimes should be studied at regular intervals.

-One should try to use all the sections in the best possible way, as per one's usage and requirement.

Planning the taxes way ahead of time, starting from the month of April of a fresh fiscal year can help one to save a lot of time, money, and effort which can help in wealth creation as well.

Tax Impact on Investments:

Investments are made either with the intention to grow the capital on investment or to save tax. Money is taxed at different stages of investment. We use EEE(Exempt-Exempt- Exempt) for simplicity where E stands for Exemption at different stages to identify the best instrument for investments where:

The first E identifies whether an investment in an instrument qualifies for a deduction or not?

The second E identifies whether the interest earned during the accumulation phase is taxable or not?

The third E identifies whether the money withdrawn in a lump sum amount (sum of the principal and returns) is taxable or not.

Other variants of EEE are:

EET stands for Exempt Exempt Taxable. Investment and received interest are non-taxable, but maturity value is taxable.

ETE stands for Exempt Taxable Exempt. Investment is eligible for an exemption, received interest is taxable and maturity value is non-taxable.

Checking the tax status of various instruments is important to identify the best instrument for investment after tax deductions, if applicable.

Rohit – "Now, Rahul you know what has to be planned before starting investments."

Rahul – "Yes *Bhaiyya*. I am now eager to know how to begin my investment journey."

Rohit – "Of course! For that, let me tell you the various investment instruments that you can use to attain it. There are two areas to invest in, first is the fixed-income instruments and the other is equity. In the next chapter, I will explain to you the fixed-income instruments that have almost fixed, stable, or less risky returns."

Activities:

1) Check how much emergency coverage you have now and how much is required ?
2) Check how much term insurance and health insurance you have now and how much is required ?
3) Check if you have your own house or own car and if you have its insurance or not ?
4) Check all the tax sections carefully which you might be eligible, but you are not using ?
5) Check whether the investment instruments you are using are under EEE/ EET/ETE category ?

Summary:

1) Emergency cover of 3-12 months should be accumulated based on your family responsibilities.
2) Health Insurance and Term insurance are mandatory insurance, even if you are having it from your workplace.
3) Vehicle insurance and property insurance are mandatory only if you own a vehicle or a property.
4) Travel Insurance should be mandatorily taken if travelling to foreign countries.
5) Effective tax planning utilizing appropriate sections helps in minimizing taxes and ultimately wealth creation.

Chapter4 :Investment Avenues

"How many millionaires do you know, who have become wealthy by investing in a savings account?"

– Robert G. Allen.

Real Estate:

Real estate investments involve the purchase, management, and sale or rental of real estate for profit. Real estate can be considered one of the safest investment instruments where people can keep getting rent and the price of property keeps on increasing under normal conditions. However, buying a property for residential purpose is never called an investment. I have seen people normally considering their own house of living as an investment too which is not the correct way to think. A house or a commercial property that people may buy to put on rent is the actual way of using real estate as an investment. When you invest in a property by taking a home loan, you can get a deduction of 1.5 lakhs in principal and 2 lakhs in interest. This helps you in tax saving as well.

Rental yield is the way to analyze the potential of real estate as an investment option. It is the annual rate of rental return, which an investor can earn from his invested capital in a property.

This further implies that investment in affordable or mid-segment projects can fetch you higher returns than high-ticket purchases. However, the probability of the same depends upon factors such as project type, location, amenities offered, level of maintenance, and the developer's brand.

The rental yield formula is Net rental yield = [(Annual rental income – Annual expenses) / Total property cost] x 100.

For Example: Property cost is Rs 40 lakhs and rent per month is Rs 10000

Net Rental Yield = ((10000*12)/4000000) *100 = 3%.

This example is a real example from a property in Pune. Similarly, rental yields in the top eight metro cities in India are as:

Delhi NCR 2.79 percent
Bangalore 3.45 percent
Mumbai 2.44 percent
Ahmedabad 3.22 percent
Chennai 3.10 percent
Hyderabad 3.16 percent
Pune 3.09 percent
Kolkata 3.96 percent
Source: 99acres

Checking on rental yield will really help one to know whether the investment will be beneficial or not.

The biggest drawback of buying a property for investment is its illiquid character as most properties take time to be sold out.

"Diversify your investments to rectify your returns."

REIT:

REIT stands for real estate investment trust. It's a great alternative to real estate. It solves the drawback of liquidity that real estate investments suffer. It works in a similar manner to mutual funds. In mutual funds, a pool of money is collected to invest in various schemes, and similarly, the pool of money is collected to invest in REITs. A Demat account is required to purchase REITs. REITs are traded just like shares or exchange-traded funds. If someone wants to invest in real estate but doesn't have large chunks of money and still wants to take the advantage of the growth in real estate, then REIT can be a good option. Here one can have ownership of the real estate for a much lesser amount, maybe even as low as Rs.300. Here diversification of real estate is possible and it is professionally managed. Liquidity is the best part and it stops all the hassles of searching for a buyer, talking to a broker, showing the property, and checking the legality and paperwork. They allow for fractional ownership depending on the amount people invest. The risk is less as 80% of the properties are completed commercial properties. Any interest or dividends received can be exempted from taxes depending on tax concessions received by REITs. These are regulated by

SEBI and cannot be started by any other person just like that. They invest in properties that are ready or more income-generating like Commercial properties, as the rent is more here. More rental yield means more profit for the investor.

90% of the rental income received is distributed to investors. Limited options of the Embassy, Mindspace, and Brookfield BRRL are available. One can even think of mutual funds that invest in REITs. REIT is one of the best options to invest in real estate with only a small amount.

NOTE: Mutual funds will be discussed in Chapter 5.

Government Securities and Bonds:

Government securities are debt products issued by the central and state governments of India. The government issues such bonds to have liquidity as they require funds for the purpose of infrastructural developments. The bonds issued by the government are called government bonds or G-sec and are issued to either fund certain development or operational activities or when it is going through a liquidity crunch. Such bonds are considered to be a lower risk as it is highly unlikely for the government to have the inadequate cash flow to falter on interest payments. The bonds issued by private organizations are called corporate bonds. The minimum amount for investment is Rs.1000 with no capping. G-sec is primarily a long-term investment tool issued for periods ranging from 5 to 40 years. Bonds have become an ideal investment instrument for investors who do not want to put all of their eggs in one basket. A basket should have an idle combination of debt and equity to effectively create a diverse portfolio of the guaranteed corpus. That's why investors look towards bonds as a steady income source over time. However, similar to other financial instruments, bonds also include risks. The best way to mitigate the risks involved is to choose AAA-rated public sector companies.

Bond prices are inversely proportional to market interest rates and are dependent on various factors such as the credibility of the issuer, maturity, and interest rates in the market.

Different types of government securities and bonds:

1. **Fixed-Rate Government Bonds:** These are issued by the government to offer a predetermined amount as interest at regular intervals.
2. **Sovereign Gold Bonds:** These are a type of bond that provides an alternative to purchasing physical gold as tradable security. The Reserve Bank of India issues SGB on behalf of the Indian government, denominated in grams of gold.
3. **Floating-Rate Government Bonds**: It has fluctuating interest rates and provides different interest payments to bondholders from time to time.

If the investors want to mitigate the risk profile to a negligible level and can wait for a minimum period of 5 years, then government bonds and securities are the ideal investment options. Such bonds are ideally suited for investors within the 30% tax bracket. Government bonds provide guaranteed pay-out and principal repayment and can be utilized as an effective addition to the core portfolio.

Gold:

Gold is the favourite investment instrument for a majority of the investing population in our country and has consistently proven to be a powerful inflation hedge. There are broadly 4 ways in which gold can be bought - Gold exchange-traded funds, gold mutual funds, sovereign gold bonds, and physical gold. When bought in physical form, safety is the biggest issue. Making charges are in the range of 5-40%. Apart from that, a GST of 3% is charged.

Gold mutual funds are a good option for someone looking to get exposure to gold with as low as Rs. 1000. Sovereign gold bonds are the best option to invest in gold, for people with sufficient time and for those who are looking for gold as an investment option. Here we get some interest every year till the locking period of 8 years currently. The amount received as capital appreciation after the locking period is tax-free.

Tax on Sovereign Gold Bond (SGB)

STCG (short-term capital gain) -- If these are sold before 3 years of purchase, the gain is added to income and taxed as per the income slab.

LTCG (Long-term capital gain) -- If these are sold after 3 years of purchase, 20% tax (if indexation) is availed, and 10% if not.

Indexation is a method used to adjust the purchase price of an investment to reflect the effect of inflation on it.

It increases the buying price of the asset, resulting in higher profits. At least 5-10% of one's portfolio should be allocated to gold as it is an evergreen commodity and will never lose its shine.

Here the investor saves on the following:

• 3% GST on the purchase of gold.

• 1% TDS which is charged if the physical gold is of more than two lakhs rupees in value.

• GST on the making charges.

• Long Term Capital Gain if held till maturity or via HUFs (Hindu Undivided Family) and Trusts.

Kisan Vikas Patra (KVP)

KVP is basically an initiative by the Indian Government to encourage small savings in our country for the investor's secure future. It is suitable for investors who are reluctant to take risks, have surplus money, and are looking for assured returns. KVP is a small savings instrument that facilitates people to invest in a long-term savings plan. Any resident Indian can invest in the KVP scheme and can obtain a certificate either jointly or individually, or in the name of a minor. It is a fixed-rate scheme designed to double your investment after a predetermined period of time. The main target audience for this scheme is people in semi-urban and rural areas. The minimum investment starts from Rs. 1000 with no maximum limit. It offers tax benefits of up to Rs. 1.5 lakh under Section 80C of the Income Tax Act, 1961. It can be bought from the nearest post office and is a good option to accumulate wealth over time without any fear or risk.

Public Provident Fund (PPF)

Anyone looking for a safe investment option to save taxes and earn guaranteed returns should open a PPF account. It enables one to build a retirement corpus while saving on annual taxes. A PPF account can be opened by an adult for themselves or on behalf of a minor. It has a lock-in period of 15 fiancial years as financial year in which the account is opened is not counted. Deposits can be made in a lump sum or in installments. The deposits must be made every financial year during the tenure and such deposits are exempted from income tax u/s 80C. A minimum deposit amount of Rs.500 per financial year is required to keep the account active. If people fail to do so, a penalty is charged. A PPF account can be opened at either a Post Office or at any nationalized bank like the State Bank of India or Punjab National Bank, etc. These days, even certain private banks like ICICI, HDFC, and Axis Bank among others are authorized to provide this facility. PPF is one investment vehicle that falls under the Exempt-Exempt-Exempt (EEE) category. This means that the principal invested, the interest earned as well as the maturity amount are tax-free. PPF is the best instrument to have wealth creation by secure means with a tax-saving option.

Sukanya Samridhi Yojana (SKY)

It is a government-backed small savings scheme for the benefit of the girl child. SSY accounts can be opened at designated banks or post offices. It has a tenure of 21 years or until the girl child marries after the age of 18. The SSY scheme comes with a higher interest rate along with several tax benefits. From a taxation perspective, SSY investments are designated as EEE investments. This means that the principal invested, the interest earned as well as the maturity amount are all tax-free. Under existing taxation rules of SSY, the tax benefit on the principal amount invested is up to Rs 1.5 lakh per annum under Section 80C. It is considered to be a good option to invest in a girl child's future requirements of higher education and marriage.

"Returns matter a lot. It is our capital".

-- Abigail Johnson

Fixed Deposit (FD)

A fixed deposit is a type of term investment offered by several banks and non-banking financial companies (NBFC). FDs are one of the most popular ways to save money. They are a safe investment, offer good returns, and are easy to start. An FD investment is valuable in many ways:

- Offers an opportunity to earn a higher rate of interest on surplus funds.
- Yields assured returns.
- Minimum duration is 7 days and the maximum is 10 years.
- Senior Citizens get a higher interest of 0.5% on the FD.
- It has the flexibility for withdrawal at the end of tenure or receives monthly, quarterly, half-yearly, or yearly pay-out.
- Highly liquid as you can withdraw the amount during the tenure also with some penalty.

- Loan can be availed against an FD in case of financial emergencies.
- Not dependent on market conditions.

During Covid19, people having fixed deposits were not impacted by the stock market condition as they knew their money is stable and they will get returns based on the fixed deposit document's terms and conditions.

People with less risk appetite can have FD for a stable portfolio.

"In investing, what is comfortable is rarely profitable."

– Robert Amott

Till now we have discussed gold, real estate, REIT, Government Security, PPF, *Sukanya Samridhi Yojana*, Senior Citizen Saving Scheme, and FDs. All these options provide stable and secure returns and are suitable for people having low-risk appetites. These investments require huge amounts to be invested for a long tenure to reach a specified goal.

Let me give you an example:

Ramesh wants to have a corpus of Rs.1 crore after 20 years. He chooses one of the investment products discussed above that gives 8% return.

For generating One crore corpus with 8% returns, Ramesh has to invest 17,000 each month for the next 20 years.

NOTE: We have not mentioned any return percentage with any product as they keep changing with each coming quarter. Here we have considered 8% which is on the higher side.

Rahul – "*Bhaiyya*, the options discussed till now require huge investment with less return. Is there any other option that can provide better returns?"

Rohit – "Yes, we have many instruments under equity for better returns. Let me explain it in detail in the next chapter."

Activities:

1) You might be having a real estate loan. If not, someone in your circle might be having it. Calculate the actual amount paid in full tenure of payment of the loan.
2) Find out the current return percentage range of the instruments discussed in this chapter.
3) Try to find the amount required for generating Rupees one crore corpus for each instrument discussed till now.

Summary:

1. Fixed income instruments give similar types of returns.
2. Fixed income instruments are suitable for low-risk appetite people.
3. The use of Fixed income instruments to create a corpus will make a steady stream of cash flows.

Chapter5 Equity

> ***" Someone is sitting in shade today because someone had planted a tree long time ago."***
>
> ***– Warren Buffett***

Equity

Equities provide you with a chance to build a diversified portfolio. It is a better option compared to the investment avenues discussed in the last chapter, as they give good returns. Equities are the best way to participate in the growth of any business by investing in it. There are different ways to invest in equities. We will be discussing the same here.

Direct stock

Direct Equity -- Investors buy stocks of companies listed in the stock exchange using their Demat account. With this, one may become a partial owner of those companies and with the growth of the company, stock prices increase. This feature helps the investor in making profits.

For Example: Suppose one buys 100 stocks of Xyz Company at Rs.100. Within a few days of purchase, the stock prices go up to Rs. 110. Then the profit that the investor will be making on it is 110-100 i.e. Rs. 10 per share. The number of shares bought has been assumed to be 100. So, the total profit comes to Rs. 1000 (100x10). Similarly, if, after the purchase, the stock price goes down to say Rs.95, then the loss the investor will be making on it is 100 -95 i.e. Rs. 5 per share. As the number of shares has been assumed to be 100 so, the total loss becomes Rs. 500 (100x5).

There are so many businesses around us and we might be a consumer to quite a few of them. One can buy the stock of any such company (if listed on the stock exchange) based on the popularity and performance of the brand. If one does not buy the stocks of a popular brand, then one might miss out on not becoming part of its growth story. We have so many people working in IT industries, pharma companies, and manufacturing industries. They know that their companies are the best in the business and yet, they do not invest in the growth story of their company and lose the profits that they could have made by investing in them. However, before investing in stocks through direct equity, there are various questions an investor needs to ask himself.

Questions like:

1. What is the business of this stock company?
2. What are the future prospects of the industry and this company?
3. Till when will I remain invested?
4. Am I investing because someone told me or do I really see value?

There are many questions like these that one needs to ask oneself before and after investing. Some people use fundamental assessments, whereas others use technical analytical methods to decide which stock to buy. If people don't want the hassles or don't have time to do such an analysis, then there are ways, as stated below, to nevertheless, invest in equities.

National Pension Scheme (NPS)

NPS is a social security initiative by the Central Government. It is a pension cum investment scheme launched by the Government of India to provide old age security to the citizens of India. One can invest in a mix of equity, government bond, corporate debt, and alternative assets. Once the decision is made on the asset mix and fund manager, the money is invested in specific schemes in these 4 asset classes.

Withdrawals from NPS can be understood as :

Withdrawal on	Lump Sum	Pension
Maturity	60%	40%
Before 60 years	20%	80%
Death of subscriber	100%	0%

The lump Sum received in any of the scenarios is tax-free income. Pension income is taxable as per your salary bracket.

It is a good scheme for anyone with a low-risk appetite and who wants to plan for retirement with a regular pension (income) in the retirement years. It is a boon for individuals who retire from private-sector jobs. A systematic investment like this can make a massive difference in someone's life, post-retirement.

The major benefits of NPS are as follows:

1) It is the world's cheapest retirement plan.

2) It is a voluntary scheme and is open to all Indian citizens falling between the age group of 18 to 60 years.

3) The scheme comes with a lot of flexibility which allows people to choose their investment options.

4) One can also switch between different investment funds.

5) The NPS account can be operated from anywhere in India.

6) The plan involves transparent investment norms.

7) It helps one to plan retirement with the assurance of receiving assured returns at retirement.

8) The investor can get additional tax benefits under Section 80 CCD.

Pension Fund Regulatory and Development Authority (PFRDA) regulates the operations of NPS. NPS contributions can be made through both online as well as offline means. NPS fund managers manage the investments and therefore the investor is spared the hassle of tracking the investments. It is a good scheme for people who want to take advantage of equity and have a low-risk appetite as well.

Unit Linked Insurance Plan (ULIP)

ULIP is another way to get the benefit of equity. It is a combination of equity and investment. By investing in it, one can invest in a mix of equity, government bond, corporate debt, and alternative assets. There are fund managers in the insurance companies who manage the investments and therefore the investor is spared the hassle of tracking the investments. ULIPs allow us to switch our portfolio between debt and equity based on our risk appetite as well as our knowledge of the market's performance. Benefits like these which offer investors the flexibility of switching is a huge factor contributing to the popularity of these investment instruments. There are several points to keep in mind before investing in any ULIP scheme. The first is to make sure that the investment in such a policy is in line with the future goal we might have in mind. What are the investment goals that we might be looking at? Since a part of the premium is going to be used for investments, and since market risks are present, does that work? If a fixed sum of money is required at maturity or death of the investor, the total investment may need to be carefully calculated. They have a lock-in of 5 years. It means money cannot be redeemed in those 5 years. Generally, ULIP plans are transparent, but it is necessary to check all the charges which will be levied. Comparing different plans offered by different insurance companies will give the option to choose the best plan. Since investment is envisaged, it is important to check everything. These are best suited for individuals with a long-term financial plan of wealth creation and insurance. Whether it is for retirement, children's education, or other financial goals, a ULIP continued till maturity works as an advantage. It gives the investor the dual benefit of savings and protection, all in a single plan.

From a taxation perspective, Ulip investments are designated as EEE investments as they have involvement of insurance. This means that the principal invested, the interest earned as well as the maturity amount are all tax-free. It is one of the best investment for individuals who are not savvy with equity but would like to get benefit from long-term capital appreciation.

Exchange Traded Funds (ETF)

ETF is a financial security that tracks or replicates the performance of an underline asset. The underline asset can be equity, index, gold, silver, sector, bonds, currency, or global index. Exchange Traded Funds are seen as attractive investment bets given their low cost, stock-like features as well as the tax exemption that some categories of ETFs offer.

They are considered to be a fusion between a stock and a mutual fund and can be sold and purchased just like any other stock on the stock exchange. The major requirement to invest in ETF is to have a Demat account.

There are several advantages of Exchange Traded Funds.

- They are considered to be quite cost-efficient.
- They allow the investors to create a diversified portfolio for themselves.
- They allow investors to enjoy tax exemptions when traded in large volumes.
- They can be traded anytime during the day when the market is open. In other words, the trading can continue throughout the day. The only issue is that we need to buy at least 1gm. of gold.

ETF is one of the most suitable instruments for investors who want to have diversification at low cost.

"Mutual funds were created to make investing easy, so consumers wouldn't have to be burdened with picking Individual stocks."

– Scott Cook

Mutual Funds:

A mutual fund is a pool of money managed by a professional Fund Manager. It is a trust that collects money from a number of investors who share a common investment objective and invests the same in equities, bonds, money market instruments, or other securities. The income/gains generated from this collective investment are distributed proportionately amongst the investors after deducting applicable expenses and levies, by calculating a scheme's "Net Asset Value" or NAV. Simply put, the money pooled in by a large number of investors is what makes up a Mutual Fund. There are fund managers who manage the investments and therefore the investor is spared from the hassle of tracking the investments on a regular basis.

Mutual funds have a full universe of funds ranging from debt to equity. They are broadly classified under the asset class:

1) Equity MF —They primarily invest in shares/stocks of different companies. They have the potential to generate significant returns over a period. Hence, the risk associated with these funds also tends to be comparatively high.

2) Debt Funds — They invest primarily in fixed-income securities such as bonds, securities, and treasury bills. They invest in various fixed-income instruments such as Fixed Maturity Plans (FMPs), Gilt Funds, Liquid Funds, Short-Term Plans, Long-Term Bonds, and Monthly Income Plans, among others. They can serve to be a great option for passive investors looking for regular income (interest and capital appreciation) with minimal risks.

3) Money Market funds -- Investors trade stocks in the stock market. In the same way, investors also invest in the money market, also known as the capital market or cash market. The government runs it in association with banks, financial institutions, and other corporations by issuing money market securities like bonds, T-bills, dated securities, and certificates of deposits, among others. The fund manager invests the investor's money and disburses regular dividends in return.

4) Hybrid funds – They are an optimum mix of bonds and stocks, thereby bridging the gap between equity funds and debt funds. The ratio can either be variable or fixed. In short, it takes the best of two mutual funds by distributing, say, 60% of assets in stocks and the rest in bonds or vice versa. Hybrid funds are suitable for investors looking to take more risks for 'debt plus returns' benefits rather than sticking to lower but steady income schemes.

Let us understand the major types of Equity Mutual funds that are widely used:

1) **Large-cap** – They invest in large companies, primarily the top 100, in teams of market capitalization.

2) **Midcap** -- They invest in companies primarily in the 101-250 bracket in teams of market capitalization.

3) **Small cap** -- It is one of the most aggressive categories of equity mutual funds because the stocks chosen under this category is of companies that are listed after the 251st rank in terms of market capitalization.

4) **Flexicap** -- there is no market cap linked restrictions for investment in largecaps, midcaps and small caps category.

5) **Multicap** – They need to have a minimum of 25% each in large caps,midcaps and small caps category.

6) **Equity Linked Savings Scheme (ELSS)** -- These are the tax-saving mutual funds that invest in equity instruments to create a sizeable corpus. These funds allow investors to reduce the taxable income by up to Rs 1,50,000 per financial year by investing that amount in ELSS funds. It has a lock-in period of 3 years which is the lowest as compared to any other tax-saving tools under section 80C.

7) **Index funds** -- Index funds are passively managed funds in which the portfolio includes all the stocks of an index. These are used to diversify the equity investments through the index to grab the overall growth and normalize the associated risks of equities.

8) **Thematic funds** -- Thematic mutual funds invest in the stocks of companies that are based on a particular theme. The theme can be international exposure, rural

India, MNC, energy, PSU, etc. A theme may comprise multiple sectors which have the same flavor. These funds are most suitable for experienced investors.

9) Sectorial funds -- Sectoral mutual funds are equity funds that can only invest in the companies which belong to a particular sector. These funds are considered risky and are suitable for experienced investors as these funds can provide exponential gains or losses depending on the market condition. Generally, most of the stocks associated with a particular sector tend to follow similar trends.

10) Value/Contra funds -- The value-oriented funds or contrarian funds are mutual funds that bet on underperforming stocks which are available at cheaper prices. These funds are risky but the right value/contra fund can give significant returns in the long term. Investors with a high-risk appetite can choose these schemes for long-term gains.

11)Large and midcap funds -- This category of equity mutual fund uses stocks of the top 250 companies listed in the Indian stock market. It is a combination of large-cap and mid-cap mutual funds. These funds invest in equity instruments of large-cap and mid-cap companies. The large-caps are stable and less risky while the mid-caps are risky but have better opportunities for growth. The combination allows investors to gain high returns in long term with a moderate to high-risk factor.

12) Focussed funds -- As per the norms of SEBI, a focused fund can only invest in a particular number of stocks belonging to a particular number of sectors. The number of companies is 20-30 in number. These funds limit the diversity in the portfolio as over-diversifying the portfolio can reduce the returns.

Few tips for Investing in Equity Mutual Funds:

1. Know Your Investment Objective: Investment in equity mutual funds must be done to achieve a certain goal. Investment objectives can be wealth creation, retirement planning, buying an asset, etc. The tenure to achieve the goal must be kept constant and the fund selection should be done accordingly.

2. Know Your Risk Appetite: Investors of equity mutual funds must know their risk tolerance level. A variety of equity funds are available in India with different risk factors. An investor must choose the one which possesses the risk that is in line with the investment objective and risk tolerance level.

3. Maintain Discipline: Discipline is the key to being a successful investor in equity mutual funds. Decisions made in a panic must be avoided. SIP investment must be continued until the objective is reached. By not investing during the bear market, an investor might miss the opportunity to buy more units at a cheaper price.

4. Stay Updated: Equity mutual funds are subject to market risks and investors must keep a track of market trends and updates. It is not essential for a SIP but better decisions can be made with the help of the proper knowledge of the market trends. If a market is falling, additional purchases can be made on SIP to maximize the output.

5. Regular Monitoring: Equity mutual fund investors must check their investments at regular intervals and make a decision to refurbish the portfolio or SIP amount if needed. If the portfolio is constantly facing loss, assistance from an expert can be taken to alter the investments.

6. Diversify your investments: Don't put all your eggs in one basket. Instead of investing all your money in one fund, it is better to spread the investment amount over a number of schemes. The chances of loss get reduced and the diversification allows consistent growth.

7. Don't Focus on NAV: NAV decides how many units will be assigned to the investor. A higher NAV does not mean a better fund or a lower NAV does not mean the growth will be faster. The growth of NAV must be checked by percentage rise or fall. 1 unit of a fund with a NAV of Rs 1000 is equal to 100 units of a different fund with a NAV of Rs 10.

8. Selection of Scheme is the Most Important Part: The selection of a mutual fund must be done after considering every aspect of a fund including volatility, the risk-to-reward ratio, experience, and strategy of the fund manager, portfolio structure, investment style, stock selection style and past performances under different market conditions. Past performances must not be the only factor to consider as a fund doesn't need to repeat what it has done in past, but it can surely give an idea of the ability of the fund.

The chance of any investor getting confused is high here as there are so many options available. So, sometimes finding a fund suiting his needs becomes an important aspect. It requires expert guidance to decide on this. Financial advisors could be the best possible available option to get help in case of confusion, as they are deft with the amendments and current scenario and are supposed to prepare or evaluate financial document summaries, investment performance reports, and income estimates for their clients.

Major difference between buying a stock and a mutual fund, that most of the people don't consider is:

Stock Price	Mutual Fund
When stock prices go down, you have to select stocks efficiently else you might get stuck with a crap stock that might not come up for various years.	When NAV comes down, you need not worry and can buy without worry as fund managers will buy the right stocks at right time.

"Courage taught me no matter how bad a crisis gets, any sound investment will eventually pay off."

– Carlos Slim Helu

After going through different instruments of debt and equity, one might have understood that every instrument has its own pros and cons. As an investor, we need to understand in and out of different financial instruments and then choose what suits our financial goals. Our financial condition and commitment differ and so the idea of any one size fitting into all strategies have no relevance. Personalized investment solution is the need of the hour and this need could be fed with the help of financial advisors. As their major role is to prepare a particular financial plan for each person and guide people throughout the investment journey. Risk-taking ability, future financial goals and investment horizon vary from person to person. They are supposed to manage clients' portfolios up to date with the requirements of the market. Most investors prefer a combination of debt and equity to have a stable and robust portfolio in different market scenarios. For deciding how much percentage of investments should be in equity and how much should be in debt, a simple formula of 100-Age can be used.

For Example: As your age is 25, 100-25 is 75. So, you can invest 75% in equity and 25% in debt instruments.

Rahul – "Thanks *bhaiyya*. Now I think I can start my investments."

Rohit – "No Rahul. Wait for a few more moments. Let me make you understand the important concept of inflation which is commonly ignored by people."

Activities:

1) Find out the current return percentage range of the instruments discussed in this chapter.
2) By using the percentage from Activity 1, try to find the amount to be invested for reaching one crore in 20 years by using each of the instruments.
3) Compare it with the last chapter chart you prepared, it will help you to choose the correct investment instrument.
4) Check your debt % and equity % based on your age.

Summary:

- Equity investments have more risk.
- The risk will be less if we understand the instrument completely before investing.
- Equity investments give better returns than fixed income instruments.
- Equity investments can create huge corpus with low amounts.

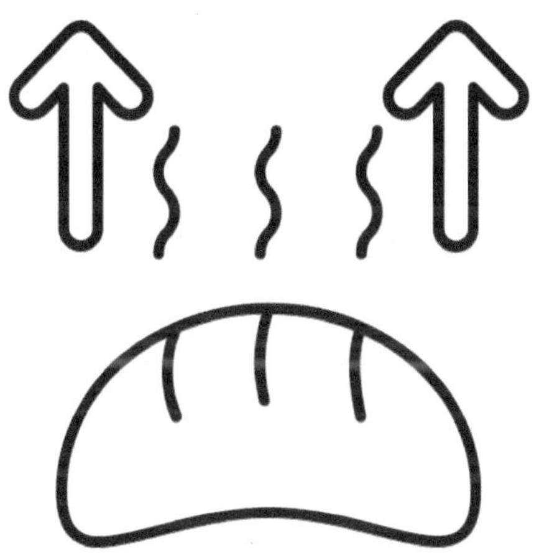

Chapter6: Inflation

" Inflation takes away from the ignorant and gives it to well informed."

– Venita VanCaspel

Rohit – "Rahul, just imagine you are a married person and you have an infant. If this would be the scenario, then how much do you think you would require for your child's education after 18 years from now?"

Rahul – "As per current statistics, as per my calculation I would require Rs 10 for my child's higher education."

Rohit – "Rahul, Rs.10 Lakhs is correct as per the current requirement but you need to consider inflation which is the most important aspect to consider before planning for investments."

Rahul – "Yes, I did not consider it as I am not aware of it, can you please explain in detail about Inflation, as I never knew it affects my investments as well?"

Rohit explains -

"Inflation is the regular increase in prices of goods and services. It makes money in your hand lose its value with each passing year. As prices keep increasing, inflation leads to higher prices and lower purchasing power.

Inflation happens because of two things:

1) Demand - Pull Inflation – Growing demand for goods and services leads to insufficient supply. If something is in short supply, you will be bound to buy it at a higher price.

For Example: In 2020, there was a global economy shut down due to the coronavirus pandemic. As the demand for Covid19 medicines kept increasing with more patients, and the supply was less, so prices kept increasing.

Demand-Pull inflation leads to cost-pull inflation.

2) Cost–pull Inflation – When raw material prices increase, businesses in turn increase the prices regardless of demands.

For Example: An increase in the cost of petrol results in an increase in transportation costs which in turn increases the cost of vegetables and other things we use in daily life.

3) Built-in inflation - As demand-pull inflation and cost-push inflation occurs, employees may start asking employers for a raise. Workers may start asking businesses for higher salaries.

Things that we are able to buy for Rs.10,000 today might require Rs.19,670 after 10 years considering the 7%

inflation rate. Similarly, after 10 more years i.e. 20 more years from now, the same item would attract a cost of Rs 38,696. This price will keep doubling every 10 years, making the price of the same item go up by Rs 1,49,744 after 40 years. These are worrying figures that warn us to plan in accordance with inflation for all future expenses. This is the reason, investments should be planned considering inflation in mind, but sadly people are not aware of it and it is often ignored resulting in financial blunders."

By now Rahul had started understanding the correct meaning of inflation and how it's impacting his life.

Rahul – "Ok, bhaiyya. Now as I have understood inflation. Can you please tell me, how much I would require planning for my child's higher education 18 years from now?"

Rohit -- "Rahul your Rs. 10 lakhs requirement would have become 55 lakhs considering 10% as the rate for education inflation."

For a few minutes, Rahul was shocked to hear the figure, but then he said: "Thanks for making me realize the correct amount that I would require. It is a staggering amount."

"The luxuries of yesterday have become necessities of today."

Lifestyle inflation:

Rahul - "Sometimes I think my expenses are increasing so much. Is this because of inflation?"

Rohit – "Yes, it is all because of the lifestyle inflation."

Rahul – "Please explain this as well to me in detail."

Rohit – "Lifestyle inflation is inflation that happens when you allow your spending to gradually increase with the increasing income over time as you desire a more luxurious and comfortable lifestyle. Lifestyle inflation is what causes people to get stuck in a cycle of paycheck-to-paycheck life where they just have enough money to pay the bills and wait for the next salary to get credited to their bank accounts.

For Example: Around 10 years back, people used to wear unbranded clothes, watches, and shoes but now most people wear branded clothes, shoes, and watches.

This is what lifestyle inflation does to you. It creates luxuries of life to become necessities. The salaries or business incomes of people have not increased at the same pace as their lifestyle inflation. So, planning a proper lifestyle to combat inflation has become very important. Below are some of the ways by which we can reduce the impact of lifestyle inflation on ourselves.

1) Calculate how much your raise is after calculating and deducting all the taxes.

2) Celebrate the rises, but do proper calculations before thinking of buying a car, or a house.

3) Be aware of your spending choices.

4) Think about extra funds towards paying loans ,credit card bills and doing investments by checking which is more appropriate.

5) Keep some percentage of increased money every month for spending extravagantly.

6) Keep a major percentage of increased income committed for long-term investment goals."

"Inflation creates a big hole in the pocket of non-planners."

Family Inflation

Rahul - "Ok I have understood lifestyle inflation. But is it the same for all people or it is different for different people?"

Rohit – "You have asked a very good question. People need to know about their family's inflation. A country's inflation can be checked by anyone by going to the government website or by various other mediums. But knowing the family inflation is important as they need to plan accordingly."

Family inflation is a form of inflation that depends on various parameters like the number of family members, the age group they are in, the requirements they have based on their current lifestyle, and the lifestyle they want to have.

For calculating family inflation, you can use below steps:

1. Check the monthly expenses of your family currently.

2. Compare it with last year's monthly expenses of your family.

3. The difference between both expenses is your family's inflation.

Fact:

After calculation, you would see that it is more than 10%. Hence planning should be done not only considering country inflation but family inflation too.

Check the age of your family members and the expenses that accrue based on the lifestyle they currently have.

Stated below are the basic expenses of various types :

Expense Type	Expenses
Housing	House Rent/Loan, Apartment maintenance charges, Property Tax, Miscellaneous expense
Utilities	Electricity, Water, Gas, Phone Bills, Cable tv, Newspapers, Internet, Misc. expense
Household	Household(Maids, cook, Driver, Nanny), House Repairs, Home appliance, curtains, linens, Carpets etc,Misc. expenses
Food	Groceries, dining out
Health Care	Medicines, Doctor consultation, Eye-care, spectacles, lenses, Regular lab tests, Dentist and dental treatment, hospoitalisation
Family Care	Child Eduction fees, Child Care – day care/care taker, Children hobby classes, Monetary Support for dependents (Parents or Children), Misc expenses
Transportation	Vehicle Maintenance and Repair, Office/School Bus Cost, Petrol/Diesel, Misc. expenses
Travel	Short Vacation, Long Vacation, Family Visits, Misc
Recreation and Entertainment	Health Club. Gym Fees, Hobby Classes, Movies and Sports Events, Dining Out (Discertionary) Misc.
Miscellaneous	Charitable Contribution, Legal Expenses, Gifts, emergency expenses

"It's not how much money you make, but how much money you keep, how hard it works for you, and how many generations you keep it for."

—Robert Kiyosaki.

Power of compounding

Compounding is the process in which an asset's earnings, from either capital gains or interest, are reinvested to generate additional earnings over time.

Compounding creates wonder in long term. Albert Einstein had once quoted ***"Compound interest is the eighth wonder of the world. He, who understands it, earns it. He who doesn't, pays it".***

When it comes to calculating interest, there are two basic choices: simple and compound. Simple interest simply means a set return percentage of the principal amount every year. Compound interest is the situation where your principal generates some returns and which is added to the main principal before investing. This creates exponential returns.

For Example:

Time period	Simple Interest(SI) @10%	Compound Interest(CI) @10%
Start	10000	10000
1	11000	11000
2	12000	12100
5	15000	16105
10	20000	25937
20	30000	67275
30	40000	174994

Here you can see, after 1 year, the amount is the same for both SI and CI. Compounding starts to be seen from the 2nd year onward. After the 2nd year, the amount of SI is Rs. 12000, but CI is Rs. 12100. It's the difference of 100 only as of now. Once this is continued for the next 5 years the amount from SI will become 15000 but the amount from CI will become 16105. It's the difference of Rs 1105. After 10 years, the amount from SI rises to 20000 but the amount from CI has now become Rs. 25937. It's a big difference of Rs. 5937. This continues and in 30 years, an amount of 10000 becomes 40000 by SI but the amount from CI will become Rs 174494. You can now see the magic of the power of compounding in longer durations. So, the earlier you start the better it will be.

Rohit – "So, Rahul by now you would have understood that our investments should be able to beat inflation and the power of compounding can create a huge corpus.

This can help you to lead a successful, secure, and beautiful life in the future with your family."

Rahul – "Yes, *bhaiya*, however, I have one question here. I have a few family members of mine. Some of them are in their '30s, some are in their '40s and some are in their 50s. Will the investment strategies be the same for all of them?"

Rohit – "No Rahul, it will not be the same for them. Let me explain the investment analysis in the next chapter."

Activities:

1) Ask your parents or any elderly person what is the minimum value they remember of anything they are still using. Compare the percentage growth from its lowest price.

2) Check the price of the shoes, watches, mobiles, and clothes you used 5-10 years back and what is their cost today. How much is the percentage growth from the previous price?

3) Check the statistics of salaries for people 5 years ago and what is it now. How much is the growth? How much is the percentage growth from the previous salary?

4) Compare and check the percentage growth in expenses and income?

Summary:

1) Inflation is reducing the purchasing power with each coming year.

2) Lifestyle inflation is hitting us unknowingly as luxuries have become necessities.

3) Family inflation is a major concern for all people and this should be taken with ultimate seriousness.

Chapter 7 Investment Analysis

"The Investments of today are the foundations of a dream life. The luxuries of today are the foundation of a disastrous life."

There is a huge meaning attached to investments. Proper investments for a trouble-free life should be one of our main pursuits of thoughts. Earning a livelihood is not enough for living. Proper investments assure us a proper life. There are many instruments and policies that promise good returns over a period. However, as mentioned before, every person has a different need and a specific purpose in life. It is important to understand various parameters of investments and returns before opting for an investment proposition.

This is an important portion of the book where important aspects of investment have been discussed, dissected, and analyzed. It is pertinent to weigh all the options and align them as per individual needs.

Investment policies:

Investment policies are bought with different investment objectives. Investment preferences depend on various things like risk tolerance, constraints on the investment portfolio, and how the investments are being managed and monitored by several companies in the market today. They are all prime examples of the same book with different covers. Presentations are different for them, but the end product is more or less the same. As personal loans come in various forms like wedding loans, travel loans, home renovation loans, pension loans, and medical emergency loans, similarly, investment policies are having different types like lump-sum amounts, pension amounts, child education policies, retirement policies, or even gradual release of funds every month/quarter/year. We as humans have emotions and we flow with that.

If we think about retirement, we take retirement or pension policy and believe that it will serve our purpose. If we have the goal of child education, we take some policies related to child education benefits. To some extent, these policies help people to get tax benefits. But what we miss calculating is the impact of inflation on our lives.

For Example: A friend, Rakesh is 30 years old and his child is 2 years old today. He and his wife want to plan for the child's graduation which will be 16 years from now. As per current costs, he plans for Rs.10 lakhs for his child's education. However, 16 years from now, the education cost of Rs. 10 lakhs will become Rs. 46 lakhs, considering 10% inflation in education.

We have already understood this concept in the last chapter on inflation. This is just a revision. Had he planned for Rs. 10 lakhs then he would have been in big trouble as the actual cost required is Rs. 36 lakhs more than what he would have planned for. This is what is happening to most of the people around us today. When asked about what was the reason for buying XYZ policy, they say - since it was a retirement policy or pension policy, or child education policy, so I bought it. The financial year was about to end, so we bought the policy for tax-saving purposes. A person who was known to me and who is an advisor has told me that it's a good policy, so I bought it. These are some common statements of most of the people. Are you also one of them?

You might have understood now what is lacking and what needs to be changed. If you are not planning the amount as per the actual requirement of the future, then somehow you will be missing big on the goals you have planned for.

For ease of analysis, requirements have been broken up as per age groups of individuals in the middle-class categories of the working population.

Rich people prioritise investments and growth, and poor people prioritise luxuries and survival.

The age group of 22-35

In the age group of 22-35, people are mostly young and they think of life to be on their toes. They think like everything will happen as they wish and think. People in this age group might be doing some job or business, going for higher education, or being homemakers for their families. We will not be considering the students going for higher education here as they are yet to start earning. But definitely, this will help them when they start earning. Most people in this age group have financial responsibilities of completing their education loan, education expenses, other expenses, and supporting their family. In this age group, they have time and energy to learn and grow in their lives. Saving some amount of money, maybe 15-20% of their take-home salaries towards building a big corpus can start from here. Instead of investing in the name of child education, child marriage, and retirement planning, they should have an amount and time period in their mind and calculate the same in consideration of the rate of inflation. As people in this age group may wonder how can we think of child education, child marriage, and retirement planning. These goals are very far. We are still very young to think about this. What is the hurry? Let's just enjoy the money we are getting. But the bigger picture is that if someone starts planning early in life, then accomplishing these goals for the future would be easier for them. They would have a long time to take the benefit of compounding and if they start in their 20s, they can actually retire in their 40s. They should have a goal amount and time period in their mind considering rate of inflation.It is this age, where a good foundation for a complete life has to be built and clear understanding of the difference between needs, desires, and luxuries has to be developed. They might have learned this from their parents at younger ages as well. But the actual implementation of it starts when you start getting money in your hands. Different people have different definitions of needs, desires, and luxuries. Getting your definitions right is very important.

When I talk to people, they say 'yes, we know what is compounding. We have already studied compounding.' But actually, they have just read about it and have not fully understood the concept of compounding to the core.

The formula of compounding is :

$$A = P\left(1+\frac{R}{n}\right)^{nt}$$

where A stands for the total amount, P stands for principal, R stands for Rate, N stands for the number of times interest is applied per time period, and T stands for the number of years or time. In this formula, 3 things are important. Principal, Rate, and Time.

In this age group of 22-35, we can utilize the benefit of time and rate. Time as we have a good number of years before retiring. We can get higher returns by taking a risk and making compounding work in our favour. Even with a small amount of money into investments, wonders can be created as they get a long time and high risk can be taken to create a sizable corpus.

For Example -- A person aged 22, if they start investing 2000rs per month for next 38 years. They can create a corpus of 1.86 crore at 12% return.

The age group of 35-50

In the age group of 35 to 50, most people are experienced enough that they start understanding the complexities of life and want to put things into planning, if not done already. People in this age group would be having children, must have bought a house, or might be planning to have one. Most of the people at this age have goals of child graduation, child marriage, retirement corpus, dream house, and dream car. In this age group, people generally have good money and energy but they have less time to enjoy the same. The definitions of needs, demands, and luxuries have already been there in mind now. Some luxuries might have become necessities in their life. But these luxuries can still be cut down by getting our priorities right. People of this age group have the maturity to understand what is right and what is wrong for them, which might not be expected from people in their 20s and early 30s. Putting some amount maybe, 15-20% of their income from job/business can help towards the proper planning of all future financial goals.

The formula of compounding is:

$$A = P\left(1 + \frac{R}{n}\right)^{nt}$$

where A stands for the total amount, R stands for Rate, N stands for the number of times interest is applied per time period, and T stands for the number of periods or time.

In this formula, 3 things are important. Principal, Rate, and Time. In this age group of 35-50, people can utilize the benefit of principal, rate, and time. People might have more money to invest after setting their priorities correctly. They still have time to take the risk and make compounding work in their favour. They might have started understanding now where they can take risks and where they cannot or should not. As their definition of risk has already sorted out by getting knowledge from various expert sources.

For Example -- A person aged 35, if they start investing 10000rs per month for next 25 years. They can create a corpus of 1.89 crore at 12% return.

The age group of 50-60

In the age group of 50-60, most people have a home loan, and their children are growing up and are on the way to their graduation. Some people who get disciplined enough or could generate more outflow of money might have finished their home loans based on their level of understanding. Some people might have started thinking of early retirement as they might not have had much energy left or they might have started having some health challenges.

People with queries in their minds fail to plan at the right time. Some of the queries are pertinent and some are not.

How my child's education will be done?

How my child will get married?

How I can have early retirement?

How I will be able to survive after retirement?

Many such questions get them puzzled every other day. They might be having a good income till now which might be going towards expenses and loans. But still, if expenses are managed properly and loans can be reshuffled or can be converted to a better rate of interest. They may still have time to make things work in the right direction. It is better late than never. They should definitely understand their mistakes now and plan things for all their financial goals. They will be having a life to survive for 20-30 years even after retirement. If not planned even at this stage, life may become difficult from here on. The formula of compounding is:

$$A = P\left(1 + \frac{R}{n}\right)^{nt}$$

where A stands for the total amount, R stands for Rate, N stands for the number of times interest is applied per time period, and T stands for the number of periods or time.

In this formula, 3 things are important. Principal, Rate, Time. In this age group of 50-60, we can utilize the benefit of the principal. People might have more money or principal from this formula of compounding to invest as they might have good earnings based on their years of experience. They need to invest a good amount of money for the proper planning of goals and make compounding work in their favor. Their risk appetite is less now as they have less time for investments and their goals will be there and have to be planned accordingly.

For Example -- A person aged 50, if they start investing 80000rs per month for next 10 years. They can create a corpus of 1.85 crore at 12% return.

All age groups

People in all age groups generally invest out of ignorance. They want to save tax, want to plan for future goals for a better future for their family and they do investments for it. They really don't do proper analysis before doing any investment. Analysis should be done and they need to ask the right questions to themselves like:

Will that be giving me the correct returns?

Will that be sufficient as per inflation?

Are the numbers supportive, by checking policy documents and what was explained by the seller of the policy?

What does the history say, if the documents have some assumptions made?

Are the interest rates declining, stable, or increasing in the longer term where the investment is planned?

What can be an alternative investment?

Can one check any other investment plan that will suit the risk appetite?

Do people need to open up their minds to learn about other investments?

Can one fulfil the goals of tax saving and wealth creation simultaneously?

If you are able to get the answers to all the questions mentioned above, then you will definitely be able to do it correctly or select better investments suiting your financial goals.

Age	Investment	Number of Years left for investment before turning 60years	Rate of Return	Corpus
22 years	Rs2000	38	12	1.86 Crores

35 years	Rs10000	25	12	1.89 Crores
50 years	Rs80000	10	12	1.85 Crores

Note : These are figures for normal retirement, if you want to retire early, Then either you need to focus on the investment amount or rate of returns.

For Example: A friend Ramesh is 25 years old. He wanted to invest. One of his associates (Rakesh) had informed him about an investment plan that generated around 8% compounding return. Rakesh had informed Ramesh that he had to invest around Rs. 17000 per month for the next 20 years to reach his goal of Rs. 1 crore. Rs. 17000 per month was quite a high amount for Ramesh. So, while pondering about it he got a chance to meet Rohit who informed Ramesh that he could meet his goal by investing just Rs. 10000 per month as it generated 12% compounding returns. Although Rs. 10000 was on the higher side for Ramesh, nevertheless, it was more manageable as compared to Rs. 17000 per month as informed earlier. This was possible as Rohit, based on his experience, had analysed the risk appetite and horizon of Ramesh and told him to invest in 3-4 mutual funds in various combinations to help Ramesh take advantage of the power of compounding and diversification.

Real estate common mistakes

The most common mistake people make:

- They love absolute numbers. They don't follow the rules of mathematics and they don't care. I bought this for Rs. 20 lahks and it is now worth Rs. 2 crore is all they will tell you. The return might be a poor single-digit number, over the long years. No one understands inflation and doesn't want to take it into consideration.

- People find an excuse to buy a property. Twenty-five-year-olds buy for settling down when they don't know where their job will take them. Thirty-five-year-olds buy for retirement, assuming they will move into a 20-year-old property when they retire. Forty-five-year-olds buy for children who won't even come back to pay society's dues. Fifty-five-year-olds buy to engage in farming, bird watching, natural living, and fresh air, who previously didn't even get out of their AC offices, or cars.
- People buy with great hope and idealist dreams. Our children will get married here; our parents will live happily here; we will retire in this place; we will sell this off if we need the money; this will only appreciate and we will be able to raise a loan against it if needed; and so on. A house enables these dreams like no other investments. People imagine and visualise these events and feel pleased about them. They almost never sell as they don't want the dream to end.
- People love the physical possession that property entails, creating a subject for lofty social conversations, without much thought on the global economy, project interest rates, or duck questions on valuation.

Instead, you should think about how much amount you have paid in the full tenure. In case you reduce or increase the tenure what will be the benefit or loss?

For Example: Aman has a Loan amount of 40 lakhs, the rate is 8% and the loan tenure is 10 years. His EMI was calculated to be Rs. 48531. In full tenure, he would have to pay Rs. 5823725 including Rs 1823725 in interest. After discussing with Rohit, Aman increased the tenure of his loan to 20 years, and now his new EMI had become Rs. 33458. The difference between new and old EMI is now Rs. 15073. In full tenure, he would be paying Rs. 8029825 including Rs. 4029825 in interest. This is like paying Rs. 2206100 more towards the loan. This is what most people calculate. However, Rohit was a person with finance knowledge. So, he suggested Aman to use the residual Rs.15073 towards investments which could generate 12% compounding returns. The total amount that Aman got after investing this Rs. 15073 was Rs. 1,50,60,146 which is roughly 7 times more than what he paid by increasing the loan tenure.

Rohit – "Rahul, now I hope you might have got an answer to your question about whether the same investment strategy can be used for all or not."

Rahul- "Yes, *bhaiyya*! Now I really want to know the exact plan for early retirement."

Rohit – "Sure Rahul, I want you to build the foundation of retirement in your mind first before going to the strategies. So, let's discuss that in the next chapter."

Activities:

1) Write down what is your age group and what are your primary goals?

2) After reading this chapter, what are the goals that have got added to your list?

3) Check your home loan total amount to be paid in complete tenure and check if by increasing the tenure and using the saved amount as an investment, how much you will be getting as a return?

Summary:

- Different goals are there for different age groups.
- There are different questions people in all age groups need to ask themselves before taking any financial decisions.
- Common real estate mistakes people do and how to correct them.

Chapter8: Foundation for early Retirement

"Retirement is a crucial goal, plan it today or repent later."

After having entered the age beyond adolescence, the primary focus of the maximum urban population is to take up a job to brighten future prospects of live and livelihood. However, earning a livelihood is only a minor fraction of meeting the requirements of life. The major part of livelihood is realized when one doesn't have to pursue the need of money. Every need is taken care of by the corpus one makes for retirement. One can make a corpus at any stage of life and retire unperturbed. During the formative years of career creation and development, one generally enters the rat race to earn and save. This is a time when one generally fails to enjoy other avenues or latent passions due to scarcity of time, intent, and money. However, retirement is the age when one can pursue other finer components of life and it is not mandatory to wait up to 60 years to be able to achieve retirement.

Retirement

The normal mindset when we hear about retirement perceives a 60-year-old person, but actually, it depends on the profession. Gymnasts can retire by 25, cricketers by 35, actors by 75, and there are politicians who never retire. Some people have forceful retirements because of their health or family conditions. You do not need to wait till 60 or a prescribed age for retirement. You can retire early too if you have your required retirement corpus. There are many people in our country without retirement funds or gratuities. Hence, the need of planning retirement becomes much more important.

Why retirement planning is necessary:

Walter Orthmann, a 100-year-old man from the southern Brazilian city of Brusque has managed to enter the Guinness Book of World Records for working at the same company for over 84 years. He explained his philosophy to the organization. "I don't do much planning, nor care much about tomorrow. All I care about is that tomorrow will be another day in which I will wake up, get up, exercise, and go to work; you need to get busy with the present, not the past or the future. Here and now is what counts. So, let's go to work!"

Source -- First post

There are many such stories that we come across every other day where people do not have plans. We may find someone in our families too, who might have had a very good life when they were working. However, after having stopped working, they struggled to even arrange for two square meals per day. For most people, their finances are defined by the salaries they receive every month. Their existence is pretty much defined by the routine of their jobs.

Max Life Insurance Company Ltd conducted a survey on retirement in partnership with KANTAR. The survey resulted that the Majority of Indians are falling behind when it comes to retirement planning, Survey has shown that India's retirement index stood at 44 on a scale of 0 to 100, indicating that Indians are lagging behind in retirement planning. Over the next 8-9 years, the number of people whose age will be above 60, will grow by 41 percent. So, planning retirement has become more of a necessity than optional.

In places like the US, Australia, Europe, and many other countries, the retirement age is increasing and it had been more than the other nations. It's only in India that people are talking about retiring at 45-50 years. However, retirement should be planned and one should have proper retirement plans considering the below reasons.

• People Don't want to work after 60 or even before that.

• It is the most crucial and costliest goal for anyone.

• Urbanization and nuclearization of families – People used to live in joint families previously. Due to improved opportunities, they have disintegrated into different cities and have more nuclear families.

• People have Less working age –The learning phase has increased to 25 recently as compared to 20 earlier and earning age has decreased now from 40 years to 35 years. Higher learning age leads to people joining the workforce late and spending less time at work. Additionally, they want to retire early as well.

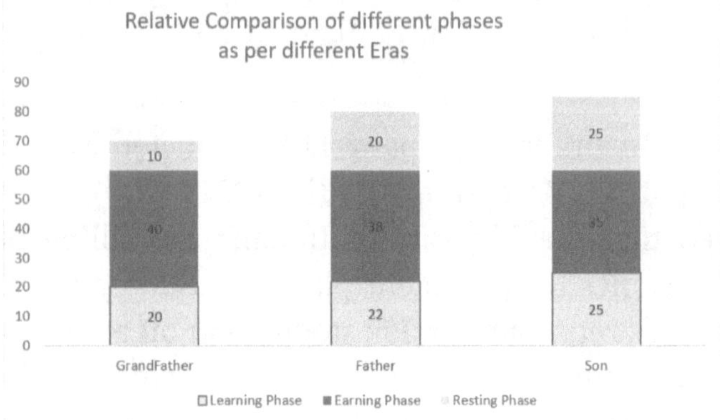

• Life expectancy has increased -- Due to medical advancements, life expectancy has increased. More life expectancy means more age to survive with the money post-retirement.

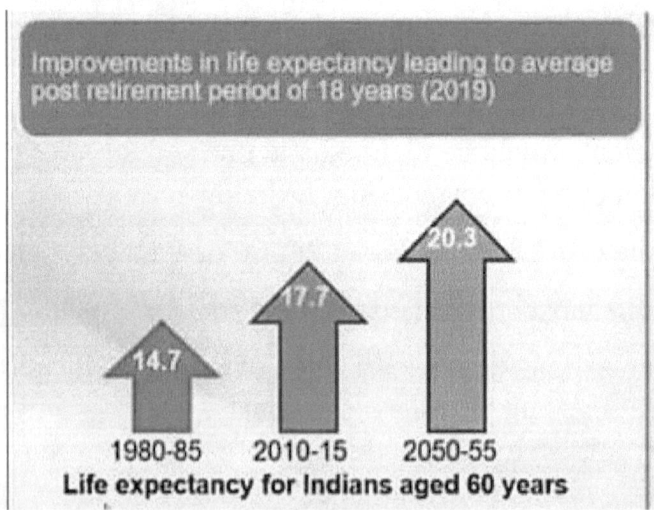

• Cost of medical facilities is rising --With increasing medical upgradation; the cost of medical facilities is also increasing. Medical expenses are set to rise around 10% p.a. in the coming years.

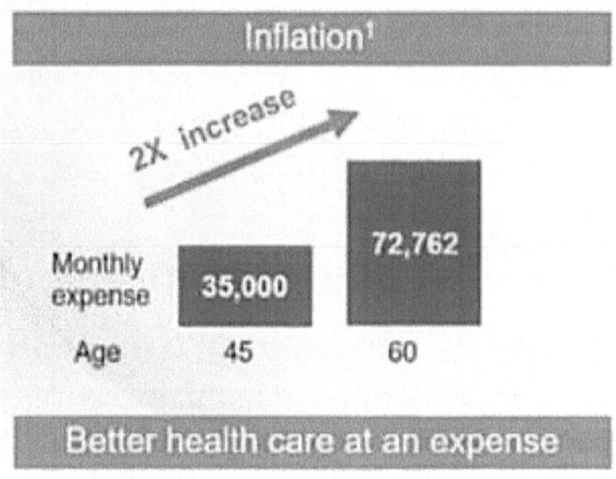

Medical expenses set to rise at 10% p.a.

• Dependency on daily activities -- People might not be able to do their daily activities independently. Activities such as dressing, feeding, washing, toileting, mobility, and transferring might require help and you might not have your children near you to take care of. They might be out of the city studying or working.

• Maintenance of current lifestyles – Proper planning is required to maintain the current lifestyle you have during your working age.

• Liquidity – People should have adequate liquidity in case of emergencies.

• Spouse support – Support of money is required for the spouse after any of the partners has lost his/her life.

• Leave a legacy – People should think about leaving a legacy for future generations, maybe children and grandchildren.

• Pension Plan – Major part of our country is not covered under any formal pension system.

• No Loan – People don't get any loans for meeting needs after retirement which they easily get in working years as they have income coming every month.

Why People don't plan for retirement?

• Most people keep retirement as their last priority – Other priorities of child education, child marriage, dream house, dream car, and dream vacations take over the most important goal of retirement planning.

• Dependency on children – Most people assume that their children will take care of them at older ages. It's good if they do so, but what if they are not able to do that because of their own priorities in life as you have yours now?

• Fear of the unknown – If you lose money in investments, it will be gone forever. You will not be able to earn more and make up for the losses. This makes most people apprehensive to take any action.

• Why to do it now – People think they are too young to start thinking about retirement. They park the thought about retirement till they are in their 50s.

How to calculate retirement corpus?

• Estimate your expenses for today. – Write down all your basic expenses of food, water, clothes, house maintenance, phone, shopping, traveling, medicine, and any other that you think will be there after retirement too.

• Check Investments, assets, and income you have – Write down all the investments, assets, and income sources you have now. From different investments how much return roughly you will be able to generate?

• Estimate your expenses after retirement – Any major goals, maybe child education and child marriage should be mentioned here. Whether they will come after retirement or else, they should be dealt with separately.

For Example: Raman has a basic expense of Rs. 50,000 per month. Considering 7% inflation, and his retirement 20 years from now. We need to know, how much he would require after 20 years from now and how much is the monthly investment. Then, we can refer to the table below:

	Present Cost	Required After (in years)	Assumed Inflation	Monthly Requirement	Yearly Requirement (Monthly*12)	Corpus that generates the yearly requirement @6%	Monthly SIP required (Assumed ROI @12%)
Basic Monthly Expenses	Rs 50,000	20	7%	Rs 1,93,484	Rs 23,21,819	Rs 3,86,96,844	Rs 39,1117

NOTE: This can be different for different people, based on their current income levels, job status, responsibilities, and many other aspects.

Common mistakes people do with retirement corpus:

1. Consuming investment funds like a provident fund, PPF for marriage, home, or other purposes.
2. They forget to get pf transferred.

3. Procrastination or not saving – Savings do not give a direct result. People want immediate results. Savings help in any emergency situation.
4. Most people don't know how much to save and invest.
5. Some people spend their retirement corpus before retirement on buying luxuries.
6. People are not concerned about asset allocation which helps by diversifying our risks.
7. Do not try to understand the implications of before and after taxes on investments.
8. Don't pay attention to health which makes them spend huge on health later.
9. They pay hefty charges to financial advisors.
10. Some people took retirement when they should have taken a break or changed their job. Leaving them with no income.
11. If people get money, they invest in gold or real estate. Very few people put it in financial assets for their long-term goal of retirement planning.

"You define your own life. Don't let other people write your script."

– Oprah Winfrey

Try to alter your glares of perception!

You can change your financial future by changing the words you use and the way you think. By changing the words and start thinking like a rich person, retiring early and being rich would be easy.

The idea itself, of thinking to be financially free or retired gives tremors in the body of people and they start doubting themselves. A few questions that directly come to mind are:

How will I be able to do it?

Is it really possible to retire early or plan for retirement?

No one in my family was able to plan early retirement. How can I even think of it?

Others are also working throughout life. I also need to do the same. Don't I?

It might require so much hard work. Will I be able to do it?

Questions like this start coming to your mind and the maximum number of people surrender to these questions. They keep working till their retirement unless they see some of their friends or known people achieving financial goals early and enjoying a better life. Normally, people don't do things or think out of the box, as no one in their immediate friend list, relatives, or colleagues were able to implement the things and make them work in their favour. They would have every other excuse to tell why they were not able to succeed and will keep stating that it was easy for the other person. These people call successful people lucky. But, deep down inside their heart, they are aware that they did not take the correct decisions or they didn't put in the right efforts to reach the financial goals they had dreamt of. Instead of cursing or being jealous of people who are ahead of you in the journey, try to be with them as it is very important to learn the mindset, they might be having because of which they were able to implement those things. It's the mindset that will make you or break you.

While our alternatives for achieving financial independence are endless, we frequently conform and see fewer options due to our pre-existing path of ideas and basis.

Do you find yourself wearing the same brand of clothes as your father? Do you have a favourite brand of coffee or tea because that's what your mother usually drank? Perhaps you lean for a particular fashion name since it was all you and your friends spoke about when you were younger. It's human nature to gravitate toward the same things our loved ones do in order to be accepted and liked, even if it puts unwanted constraints on us. To get a broader perspective, we need to shift our trance to have a clear view.

Change the thought process from

Will I be able to do it?

to

Why I cannot do it?

Never ask life, "*Why me?*"

Rather say, *"Try me!"*

Remember, if it is done by at least one person in this world, then you can also do it.

How to get positive beliefs

- Belief is what makes you take the first step and then life unfolds its magic. This has been mentioned in "The Secret" book and by all the celebrities or the people, you admire today.

So, just start with basic steps and keep working on them to create a different version of yourself.

• Check you are listening to whom:

Is that a person who has already achieved the goal?

Is that a person, you feel has a positive spark and will definitely achieve the goal?

If that person is not in any of the above categories, then that person will not be helpful in changing your thought process for making better changes in life. Such people will always be cribbing, crying, cursing, and have a jealous mindset which has never helped anyone in achieving their goals.

"The possibility of today was a dream yesterday."

Visualise

To get started, imagine your dream life, How do you want it to be? Be as specific in the details as possible. You might have fantasized to relax on the beach of Maldives, driving your dream car (Ferrari), spend a vacation with family in Paris. For effective results, go to a calm place, where there is no sound at all, close your eyes, put the ear buds, take a deep breath, and refer to the below link:

https://spotifyanchor-web.app.link/e/IPZJszmxowb

Else read the below lines imagining each word as a truth of today.

Imagine yourself in the bedroom of your dream house, waking up to the sound of birds chirping or the splash of water coming from the waterfall nearby. If you have your pets - a dog or a cat, imagine they are licking you.

I want you to close your eyes and feel the breeze coming in from the window. I want you to feel the softness of the bedsheet, and how soft the mattress is. As you wake up and stretch, what time is it? How is your bed, is it rectangular or square? What is the colour of the carpets or ceilings, who is there beside you? You say good morning, to your husband/wife/children who are just next to you with a smile, welcoming the new day. As you wake up, I want you to imagine yourself going for a walk outside. As you go out of the room, what does your home look like? You have some amazing furniture and the dining table may be from Pepperfry, home centre, or any other brand that you might have always imagined or seen in some magazine or a friend's place. An amazingly designed kitchen with a glistening granite slab. Walk through your house, and notice everything that you see. Notice the smell and sounds around you. If you have kids, listen to them as they play happily. As you walk outside, go to the terrace and see everything that you can. I want you to visualise every minute aspect in detail. Do you see a swimming pool outside? Do you see a beautifully maintained garden along with the pool with an edge-to-edge beautifully cut grass with a few mounds to enhance its splendour? I want you to get ready for your office now. What clothes would you like to wear? the brands you have always dreamed of, maybe in an Armani suit. You see yourself getting dressed in the best quality clothes of your dream brand. You are now having breakfast with your family. What kind of aroma you are getting from the breakfast, what has the chef made for you, may be your husband or wife made it for you. Visualise the smile on the face of your family while they eat it with you.

You are now going to work. Which car do you own or how many cars do you own? You select to go in which car. Which one is it, is it a rolls Royce, A Ferrari, A Mercedes, or any other car that you have always wanted to have? Which color is it? You see the driver coming out and asking you, do you want to leave for the office. You hand him your briefcase, and files and you say, yes. He opens the door for you and you step inside. Imagine for once the sophisticated-designed car and its luxury from the inside.

As you go on the way to the office, you experience the luxury of your car and are happily enjoying your way to the office, watching the views outside the mirror glass of your car. You reach your amazing workplace, It's an amazing office, with tons of supportive people, and an amazing team working towards making your dreams come true. You are the boss and you admire your employees. They are your biggest fans. See the impact you are creating from the work that you are doing.

After leaving the office, I want you to visualize the place where you are going and how you are giving back to the world. You have a charity organization, an NGO, or an old age home, You go to that place, you get out of the car, you meet the children or the old people who live there, You can see in their eyes, the love and respect they have for you, the gratitude they have for you. People are having tears watching you, as they come to know that you are the one who has created a difference in their lives. You can feel the gratitude coming from them. You can feel the impact you are making in this world. Such a beautiful and mesmerising life, isn't it?

Now, I want you to imagine or visualize going shopping one day in your amazing car, You are walking inside a mall, visualise yourself purchasing a gadget, or clothes based on your likes, you don't have to look at the price tag, See the freedom that comes with it, you can get anything that you want, it's the freedom of choice, freedom of wealth. Imagine you ask your spouse, mother, father, or anyone you love, to buy anything that they want. Maybe the most expensive thing, see the love and pride in their eyes, noticing who you have become, from where you began, and how far you have reached.

Now, you are heading towards your dream 5-star hotel where you have hosted a party for your near and dear ones. When you enter the hotel, the chef comes to greet you, he exactly knows what are your favourite dishes, and you have a great party with your loved ones and now you are on your way back home.

After reaching home, You have some entertainment in your lavish house and start packing for the vacation that you are going with your family/friends/ anyone you wanted to go for a long time at a favourite destination of yours, maybe Paris, Maldives, Switzerland or any of your dream destinations.

Now, you are hugging or curdling the person you love, you both feel proud of the life that you have created for yourself and your family, and you feel tons of gratitude for the people who have been part of this journey.

You are now going for a peaceful deep sleep for having a beautiful day waiting for you.

Now, once you open your eyes, you might be having tears or you might be in an adrenalin rush to have seen all your dreams come true.

Think about what you need to do to achieve your dream life. Make a list of steps, required to reach early retirement or financial goals of the dream car, dream house, dream vacation, and comfortable life with family. Try to be realistic, but at the same time, don't hold yourself back from dreaming big. Once you dream big, you could be able to put effort to turn them into a reality.

Perform a self-assessment

A self-assessment of your achievements so far gives you a starting point for your life plan. Look for the lessons learned and experiences you don't want to repeat. Identify your strengths and weaknesses. While doing self-assessment, ask questions to yourself on different areas of finances including the following:

- Am I having adequate emergency corpus with me?
- Am I having all the required insurance?
- Are my loans managed properly?
- What are my financial goals and are my investments aligned with them?
- Is my tax planning/saving correctly done?
- What are other sources of income I have?
- Am I analysing my current investments and making changes from time to time based on the modifications and changes in the goal?

Rohit: "Rahul, let us understand each of these questions in detail in the next chapter which will actually help you to retire early."

Activities:

1) Think and write the things that you think might have missed, if you don't plan retirement now.

2) Make a vision board with all the pictures of how you might look retired, how your house will be, what car you will have, and every other detailed specification, and keep it in the room where you spend most of the time.

Summary:

1) Retirement is the most crucial and costly goal. Its planning should be done with utmost importance.

2) Change your self-talk and think about possibilities in everything.

3) Visualise and feel the life you would be living, once you have planned early retirement properly.

Chapter 9 Strategies for early Retirement

"The earlier you plan your retirement, the easier your life would be."

Retirement planning is arranging for a consistent flow of funds after retirement. It means putting money away and investing with the objective in mind that this money would support you to sail your boat during the tides of old age. Your retirement approach will be determined by your ultimate objective, income, and age. Growing elderly can be costly. While frivolous expenses may be reduced, medical bills are likely to grow. When you include the weight of inflation, not having enough money to cover future needs can bring stress and worry. The goal of a retirement investment plan is to provide financial security in your later years without relying on others. The sooner you start, the better it would be for you. Although young people in their twenties may not be concerned about retirement, starting early allows for more flexibility. If you missed the bus, you can pick up where you left off.

A good retirement plan should be divided into three phases: investment, accumulation, and withdrawal. You should concentrate on investing and building your corpus until you are in your early 50s. As you approach retirement, you should be able to convert the money to safer investments so that you can rely on it after retirement. Many individuals do not consider insurance to be an important aspect of retirement planning; nonetheless, it is a critical and necessary component. Life insurance protects a surviving spouse. If you are no longer present, your spouse may face financial difficulties on their own.

Have Emergency corpus

Savings is a type of capital that you have in your bank account. This should be handy in case of emergencies, as in that situation, you would be requiring immediate funds. In the chapter on planning, you already read about the emergency cover and its importance. Plan your emergency cover of 3-12 months for effective planning. It can be decided based on your current responsibilities:

- If you are Just 25 years old and earning, having no dependents. Then keeping 3 months expenses corpus will be sufficient.
- If you are having a family with children, parents. Then keeping 6/9/12 Months expenses will be a better plan.

This will not only prepare you for any emergency by giving you confidence that everything is covered in life but it will also stop you from going into a cycle of the debt trap. Most people don't have emergency cover and they keep taking loans, making them land in the cycle of a debt trap and it becomes very difficult to get out of it. This mistake of theirs makes them go away from their dream of early retirement.

> ***"Good financial habits provide a dream life. Bad financial habits bring a disastrous life."***

Have mandatory and required Insurance.

Insurance is a way to manage your risk properly. There are different types of insurance currently available like term insurance, health insurance, vehicle insurance, property insurance, and travel insurance. Term and Health Insurance is the mandatory insurance for all so that your family is secured in case of any mishappening or any medical emergency. Similarly, other insurances like vehicle insurance, property insurance, and travel insurance are the required insurances and they should be on a need basis. In case you have a vehicle, go for vehicle insurance. If you have a house, go for property insurance. If you are travelling abroad, go for travel insurance. The importance of these insurances and how they should be planned is mentioned in chapter 3 under planning. We should have all the insurance in time else in case of mishappenings, this can create a big damage to your pocket as you might be bound to take a loan or break your investments. This will destroy all your future goals as well. So, planning on time is essential.

Manage your Loans

The loan is an instrument used when you don't have the amount to manage a need of yours. In such cases, you take the amount from a bank or any other Institution. Before thinking of any loan, you need to ask these questions to yourself.

Is this loan going to create an asset or liability for me?

Am I taking a loan for a need or demands/luxuries of my life?

Is this really needed?

Will I be able to manage the loan?

Will I still have the scope for investments for all other future goals?

Am I buying a house, as I want, or it's because of peer pressure?

It should be joint or single-owned?

Is there a better loan product available at lower rates?

Which home loan tenure will be beneficial for me- 5/10/20/30 years?

If I increase my tenure and use the difference for investment, will it be beneficial?

These are some of the major questions people should definitely ask themselves before taking a loan. However, I have hardly found people thinking all this before taking a loan.

I will share the story of my friend, Rakesh.

One day, I was discussing with him his future goals in life. To which he replied that my current situation itself is not sorted out, and I am not sure how to think of the future. After a few days, I got a notification on Instagram that he bought a new car worth Rs.10 lakhs. When I called him to congratulate him, he asked me whether it was the right decision or not. I am no one to comment there, but based on my discussion with him in the past, it seemed to be a big blunder. As he shared that he was struggling with his present and he bought a car that was probably not needed as his earlier car was working perfectly fine for him, giving him superb mileage, and did not need a hefty sum for the regular services. On the other hand, his new SUV was more like having a white elephant that pleased the eyes but was an encumbrance to the pocket.

For many people, this might be happening today as well. You need to ask yourself; if you just want to live a life to show off to others or if you really want to live a well-balanced life today and tomorrow as well. People just think of short-term pleasures by sleeping unnecessarily, not working hard, chit-chatting just to pass time, and unnecessarily spending time watching the OTT platform. Though they might be getting short-term profits but they are incurring much greater long-term losses which they realize later in their lives.

Many people today, take loans just because they received a message or it was readily available to them. They do not calculate how much they will pay in the complete tenure by taking that loan. People today have a series of loans and sometimes I have even seen people having many loans which have been equivalent to their current salary as well. So, you can understand what type of situation they will have in their future life.

Plan your taxes

Tax planning, Tax Avoidance, and Tax evasion are often misinterpreted by people. But these are totally different things.

Tax planning is a way to plan your taxes in a better and more efficient way. Here we are effectively saving taxes by effectively using deductions and exemption. There is no violation of law but efficient utilization of deductions, exemptions available.If you are not planning the taxes efficiently, then some or the other way, you are paying unnecessary taxes based on whichever tax bracket 10%, 20%, or 30% you are in. In the chapter on planning, you have already read how to plan taxes in an efficient manner using the different sections.

Tax avoidance is the use of legal methods to reduce taxable income or tax owed.

Tax evasion is an illegal activity in which a person or entity deliberately avoids paying a true tax liability. Those caught evading taxes are generally subject to criminal charges and substantial penalties.

If your income is less then 7.5 lakhs then you can choose new tax regime without a second thought. But if your income is more then 7.5 lakhs then you need to check which all exemptions and deductions you will be claiming to decide which tax regime is better for you. In the latter case, to save the taxes, you need to adopt the old regime which would be a better and wise option to choose from.

We could better understand effective tax planning with the help of example by taking the figures which might be used while filing an income tax return.

Assume a CTC of 16 lakhs, Here Basic salary will be 50% of the annual CTC of 16 lakhs, ie. 8 lakhs.

Annual CTC	1600000
Exemption of Employer's Contribution (12% of basic of 8 lakhs)	-96000
Gross Salary	=1504000

Exemptions

Exemptions under Section 10 on Gross Salary	1504000
HRA (25% of CTC)	-400000
Leave Travel Allowance	-50000
Prerequisites (If any)	0
Net Salary	=1054000

Deductions to find taxable income

Deductions on Net Salary of 1054000	
Section 80C	-150000
Section 24 Loss from House Property = Rent – 30% Rent – Property Tax – Interest	-200000
Section 80CCD(1B)	-50000
NPS employers Contribution	-105400
Section 80D For self and immediate family	-25000
Section 80 D for Senior Citizen Parents	-25000
Section 80 TTA (Interest on saving account)	-10000
Taxable Income	=429960

In 2022-23, Individuals earning equal to or less than Rs. 5 lakhs annually are eligible for tax rebate under Section 87A, making the tax liability NIL. Every penny saved in taxes can be utilised for investing which in turn will increase our retirement corpus too.

With escalating living and healthcare costs, many senior citizens are now facing the challenge of outliving their retirement resources. People frequently overlook the fact that retirement savings taxes and inflation can steadily deplete their corpus.

As a result, for retirement planning, it is critical to evaluate the tax advantages provided by various investment instruments. If you only consider returns, you may miss out on opportunities. Learn how to optimise the tax advantages of your retirement funds.

We should use ethical ways only to save our taxes. Using unethical ways may land us in trouble later, if not today.

In the chapter on planning, you already read about the tax planning sections and how they can be used effectively. If we plan our taxes effectively, it will help us to save money and invest that money towards wealth creation.

Plan your Investments

Investment is a way you can put money into different assets and gain some capital appreciation along with wealth creation. We should plan our investments in a proper way so that we can achieve all our future goals of child education, child marriage, retirement planning, dream house, dream car, dream vacations, and many such goals.

You should link investment instruments with all the goals you have currently, by deciding the required amount, considering inflation in mind. Starting early will help your investments to grow and will provide for sufficient amounts on maturity as compounding works better when given time. In the previous chapter, we have already come across why retirement needs to be planned way ahead of time, instead of waiting for the last 5 years before retirement.

For Example: There are two friends Mahesh and Kamlesh, both 24 years old. Both wanted to retire by age of 50.

Mahesh was serious and wanted peaceful and early retirement. So, he started investing Rs. 10,000 every month. With a 12% compounding return, he was able to generate Rs. 2.2 crores in the next 26 years the total investment being Rs. 31.4 lakhs.

Kamlesh, on the other hand, kept enjoying his life and did not do any investments. When there were only 10 years left before his retirement, he thought it was high time to make some investments for retirement. He wanted to meet the goal, so he started to invest Rs 80,000 every month for the next 10 years. His total investment became Rs. 96 lakhs but still he was unable to match the returns generated by Mahesh. This shows the importance of the time period in the power of compounding.

	Age	Every month investment	Age	Every month Inverstment	Age	Total Investment	Total Corpus
Mahesh	24	10000	40	10000	50	31.2 lakhs	2.2 crore
Kamlesh	24	0	40	80000	50	96.0 lakhs	1.9 crore

Morale: Start early and get more returns on maturity.

Check Risk-reward ratio

Today, there are various instruments available in the market to invest. As an investor, our goal should be able to check the risk-reward ratio. It varies from person to person based on age, gender, marital status, the place they live in, people in the close circle (friends, family, and relatives), the era in which they were born, and various other parameters as well. Every instrument has different rules to play just like a game. Understanding all the rules of the game makes it easier for anyone to play it. Similarly, try to understand any investment instrument deeply, before thinking to invest in them. Risk- reward ratio of the instrument should be favourable to you as an investor, and only then you would be able to reap the benefits of that instrument properly.

For Example: Anshul is in his late 50s and has 2 more years before retirement. He thinks about investing the amount in equity. This will be a bad decision for him as the risk-reward ratio will not be favourable for him. Anshul's friend, Aakash is 31 years old and has more than 20 years of retirement. Aakash can think about investing in equity with a long-term lock-in of 15 years as well, as he has sufficient time.

Do proper Investment analysis

Investment analysis is a way to analyze investments already done in the past. With every passing year, our goals of investing might also change. As goals keep changing, analysing and making changes in old investments become highly important. In the current world, everything happens very fast. As far as investments are concerned, we need to be at the tip of our toes to make changes as the impact of government policies, economic policies, and global changes can have a big dent in your portfolio. On 17th January, Nifty 50 was at 12352 and within 3 months on 3rd April, it made a low of 8083. For most retailers, it was a big loss. But all real investors wait for such moments to buy things at discount. It was like the stock market had some big billion-day sales at that time. Hence, investment analysis plays a very important role in maximizing the returns in a true way. If you don't have time and interest in this, you should definitely try to take some professional help or develop an interest to learn about these things. This will really help you to have good returns for your investments. If you don't analyse the investments, then you are just leaving things to destiny and it might land you in big trouble in the future, as returns might not meet expectations. Just take control of your life by taking control of your investments.

For Example:Rakesh and Ramesh are two close friends, who completed their graduation in 1986 and started working then on. In 1986, they started investing in PPF with Rs. 100/month. At that time PPF interest rate was 12%. Let's assume the return is the same 12% for complete tenure although it has declined now. In the next 30 years, the investment of 36,000 becomes Rs 3,52,991. In 2016, One day Ramesh just checked the latest PPF returns and he was surprised to see that PPF returns have drastically come down to 8%. So, Ramesh told Rakesh to change the investment instrument. But Rakesh did not take this seriously and he continued with the old investment. Ramesh changed his investment instrument to another giving him 12% compounding return. After 7 years, Rakesh and Ramesh both checked their investment returns. Rakesh with 8% return on his old investment had Rs

5,78,816 in 2022. When Rakesh asked Ramesh about his returns, he was surprised to hear that Ramesh's total amount had accumulated to be 7,33,183 - a difference of Rs 1,54,367.

Year 1986	Investment Each month	PPF	Year 2016	Current Investment	Year 2023
Rakesh	Rs 100	12%	Rs 352991	PPF continued @8%	Rs 578816
Ramesh	Rs 100	12%	Rs 352991	SIP investment @12%	Rs 733183

Moral: Investment analysis done on regular basis can make a big change in the total corpus. Investing on a regular basis rather than attempting to time a lump sum investment might assist you in becoming a more disciplined investor. You are compelled to invest whether the price is high or low. This removes some of the emotion from investing while also avoiding any delays in putting your money to work. You can start with small amounts. You don't need a large budget to invest in a monthly investment plan. Money is one of the primary advantages of a long-term investment strategy. Keeping your stocks in your portfolio for a longer period of time is more cost-effective than buying and selling frequently since the longer you retain your investments, the fewer fees you must pay.

Concept

Investment analysis is a way to analyze investments already done in the past. With every passing year, our goals of investing might also change. As goals keep changing, analysing and making changes in old investments become highly important. In the current world, everything happens very fast. As far as investments are concerned, we need to be at the tip of our toes to make changes as the impact of government policies, economic policies, and global changes can have a big dent in your portfolio. On 17th January, Nifty 50 was at 12352 and within 3 months on 3rd April, it made a low of 8083. For most retailers, it was a big loss. But all real investors wait for such moments to buy things at discount. It was like the stock market had some big billion-day sales at that time. Hence, investment analysis plays a very important role in maximizing the returns in a true way. If you don't have time and interest in this, you should definitely try to take some professional help or develop an interest to learn about these things. This will really help you to have good returns for your investments. If you don't analyse the investments, then you are just leaving things to destiny and it might land you in big trouble in the future, with returns not meeting expectations. Just take control of your life by taking control of your investments.

Create Multiple Source of Income (MSI)

THINK OF YOUR INCOME AS A TABLE

On the left side of the above image is a table with only one leg. If that leg breaks off, the table will collapse.

On the right side is an image of a table with multiple legs. If one leg breaks, the table will wobble, but still, stand somehow.

You can think of your life as a table and the legs as your income stream. You need to set yourself with multiple income streams so that your life doesn't collapse if one fails.

There are 7 different ways to earn multiple sources of income:

1) Earned Income – Income from jobs/Side hustle. By being active, whatever money, you make is called earned income. This is the most common source of earning for the majority of people by doing a job or working for someone else. This definitely helps other people to become richer day by day as you work harder for your income and other person makes huge profits out of it. It is nothing wrong or right. But, there are other ways to make your earned income for you. You can start a business of your interest. Owning your own business gives you the

potential to make far more money than you could ever earn working for someone else. Of course, it takes a lot of hard work, dedication, and time to build a successful business in the starting few years, but it can very much reward as you will enjoy working here being your interest area. This will be very much satisfactory and beneficial in long term both financially as well as for your personal life.

2) Dividend Income – Income from stocks, mutual funds, and ETFs that are held in brokerage accounts. You can buy stocks/ mutual funds/ ETFs based on your analysis. Whenever the underlying stocks make profits, you get dividends out of it. It is not compulsory but there are various good dividend-providing stocks. It's the best form of passive income because you don't need to do anything other than reinvest the dividends you have received.
3) Rental Income – Money earned from renting out properties. The properties may be residential apartments/duplexes, commercial real estate, or storage units. It is the best way to earn passive income.
4) Royalties – These are payments made to you for letting someone use your products, ideas or processes. You even get royalties for the use of your intellectual property, such as patents, copyrights, and trademarks.
5) Business Income – It is the income you make from running a business.

   Types of businesses you can start:1111111

   I. A service-based business: This is a business where you provide a service to customers. Exa`mples of service-based businesses include babysitting, pet sitting.

II. A product-based business: This is a business where you sell products to customers. Examples of product-based businesses include online stores.

III. A franchise: This is a business that is based on an existing business model. Franchises are popular because they offer a proven business model and support from the franchisor. Examples of franchises include McDonald's, KFC, Haldiram etc.

IV. Online business: This is a business that can be operated entirely online. Examples of online businesses include blogging, drop shipping, and affiliate marketing.

6) Interest Income – It is the money you get from lending your money to someone else. Investing in banks, bonds give you interest. It is a great way to generate passive income because you can earn money without having to do any work!
7) Capital Income – It is the money made by selling an asset for more than you paid for it, some of the prime ways can be a house, land, or stocks. Example – You bought a house at 10 lakhs and sold it at 30 lakhs. 20 lakhs is the capital income.

Concept.

MSI is a way that you have income coming in from different sources and you are not dependent on just one source. You should think about it because dependency on one source of income may be a problem in case of recessions, mis happenings, job loss, or a medical condition making you bedridden for a year or so. Even if a source has started giving you just Rs.100, that can be counted as a source of income for you. The income that you generate from multiple sources can be invested toward getting better returns. Also, MSI gives you the time and freedom to live life on your terms and with your choices. You must be able to live within your means. You must either spend less or earn more money to increase your riches. With inflation and rising costs, cutting costs can be very tough. If you can't lower your spending any further, adding another source of income will help you cover more expenses while also increasing your savings and investments. Inflation has raised the expense of living. The most affected are basic necessities such as gas and grocery prices. Adding a second source of income can help pay for greater day-to-day expenses. You'll have more money for necessities, as well as savings and investments. Also, MSI gives you the time and freedom to live life on your terms and with your choices.

Adding a second source of income can help pay for greater day-to-day expenses. You'll have more money for necessities, as well as savings and investments.

Rahul – "Thank you, *bhaiya* for giving me so much time and valuable information. Now, I have started imagining how my life would be after retirement and what things I need to take care of before it."

Activities:

1) Check different loans you hold currently with the loan percentage.

2) Check your interest area and how you can convert your interest area to generate income.

3) Make a list of instruments that you understand and you really think will be worth investing in.

Summary:

1) Insurance should be planned well ahead of time.

2) Emergency cover of 6-12 months should be maintained.

3) Investments should be done considering inflation in mind.

4) Understand the risk-reward ratio before investing in any instrument.

5) Investment analysis helps you to make changes in time and choose the right investments.

6) Tax planning should be done with the purpose of tax saving and wealth creation.

7) Multiple sources of income give you more stability as you are not relying on only one source of income.

Chapter 10: Life after Retirement

"Retirement means doing whatever I want to do. It means choice."

–Dianne Nahirny

Retiring young is everyone's dream, but for many people, it remains a pipedream only because they don't work and plan for it. Retirement planning should be done at a younger age so that you can retire early and will have the energy to enjoy the corpus you build over the years.

Retirement from work was usually considered a resting phase of life, owing to old age and the limitations of leading an active life. The world has changed in recent years, both intellectually and technologically. With the passage of time, we have made great development as a society. Retirement is now recognised as a whole new chapter with a well-planned opportunity to live life to the utmost. Retirement is not the destination; it is the journey to what comes next.

It is your chance to recreate yourself and live the second part of your life with meaning.

I interviewed Datta Tule (Internet Marketer and Entrepreneur) on his journey toward financial freedom. He belonged to a farmers' family where managing food twice a day was a challenge in itself. When he was in the 6th class, he started working to meet his family's daily needs. He was an average student and seeing his academic performance, his parents did not have many expectations from him. But he had a very good habit of reading books. In one of the books of Robert Kiyosaki "Cash flow Quadrants," he read that you need to be an investor and business owner to have financial freedom and be able to retire young. This got into his head and he started working towards it.

When he got his first job at Accenture, he was very happy. But at the same time, he had a very clear mind that after 10 years he would retire from the job. During these 10 years, he focused on his investments by increasing his financial intelligence. He lost money in various quick-rich schemes as well which he suggests people should avoid as he mentions that there is no shortcut to success. While doing his job, he kept his learning curve towards becoming an entrepreneur and a business owner which helped him to get financial freedom

Currently, he owns multiple businesses of cattle feed, a digital agency, Internet marketing, etc. He is also an investor and keeps investing towards his financial growth as it's a must according to him. He believes in diversification and investments in different asset classes of real estate, gold, stocks and mutual funds for the long term. He says, he will be a lifelong learner and suggests people to learn from their mistakes and not repeat them. He has immense discipline and a tough mindset of investing every month. He suggests you should be ready to grab the opportunity whenever it comes, maybe in equity or whatever you do. He believes, his virtue of taking risks (without risk no major gains) and clear vision of goals were the prime reasons he was able to retire 2 years before he thought he would. He mentions having a clear vision of goals in the next 1 year, 5 years, and 10 years is very important. He has created such wonderful businesses that even if he does nothing for the next 5-10 years also, he has sufficient money for all his expenses.

"The goal in life is not to try and live forever, but to create something that will be forever in people's hearts."

-- Karon Waddell

Elders must embrace retirement as a life-changing experience. After spending their entire lives completing tasks, this is a significant shift from being excessively active to excessively idle. At the same time, retirement allows individuals to live their lives as they please, using the important time they have available to pursue the interests they have always desired. Willingness and intent, combined with an equal degree of forethought, will make this lovely stage of life worthwhile. After retirement, you can start doing things that you like or love to do but its also about doing those things that you were not able to do in your working age; It might be farming or gardening, spending time with your family, having a long vacation or learning any new skill that you always wanted to, for a long time. Due to medical advancements, the life expectancy of people has increased as compared to the past. Life is a magnificent gift from God. If you have a positive attitude toward life, everything you experience and feel may be wonderful and joyful. Everything is determined by your mental process and mindset. As the expression goes, "age is just a number." Although the official retirement age is 60, you can still be young at heart after that age. To have a comfortable life after retirement, let us discuss a few strategies and investment instruments:

Three Bucket Strategy

In this strategy, you create three different buckets of investment corpus. Each bucket has its own objective as follows:

- Liquidity bucket - This bucket essentially ensures that expenses for the next 1-2 years are taken care of. Returns are secondary here, hence products like liquid funds, auto-sweep fd's are best suited here
- Medium-term basket - This basket will take care of the second leg of your retirement. Once the liquidity bucket is near exhaustion, the idea would be to gradually move investments from this bucket to the liquidity bucket. Ideally, 2-5 years of expenses can be held in this bucket. The investment decisions of this bucket would solely depend on how much you put in the liquidity bucket.
- Wealth creation bucket - After investing in the first two buckets, the balance of the money would be invested here. Essentially, investments would be made in equity to generate higher long-term returns. As you age, the propensity to consume will come down and at the same time, expenses related to healthcare may go up. The growth of the retirement corpus must be greater than the

withdrawal rate in the initial years. So initially, the retirement corpus will go up. As the expenses go up due to inflation, a time will come when the retirement corpus starts coming down. This will be the long-term investment bucket that will be invested to generate inflation-beating returns over the long term. This is an important bucket to be focussed on with the other two buckets. After retirement, you also need to survive for 20-30 years.

All the 3 buckets have their own importance. So, do not miss out on any of them as this might unnecessarily cause trouble to you.

For the above buckets, you can consider the below-mentioned schemes:

Senior Citizen Savings Scheme (SCSS)

SCSS is a government-backed savings instrument, launched with the main aim of providing senior citizens in India a regular income after they attain the age of 60 years. Some of the main benefits of the scheme are:

- Tax benefits are provided.
- Safe to invest in the scheme.
- Premature withdrawal is allowed.
- The account can be transferred across the country
- High-interest rates are offered

SCSS gives guaranteed returns on a quarterly basis. The maximum amount you can invest in an SCSS account is ₹30 lakhs. Investments up to ₹1.5 lakhs qualify for deduction under section 80C. The interest earned is added to your income and taxed as per the applicable slab. One can avail Senior Citizen Savings Scheme through certified banks and post offices in India. For an investor of 60 years, this can be the best instrument to meet the post-retirement needs of an individual.

Pradhan Mantri Vaya Vandana Yojana (PMVVY)

It was launched with the main aim of providing senior citizens in India a regular income after they attain the age of 60 years. This policy was introduced by the government and run by LIC for providing pensions to people. You can invest up to Rs. 15 lakhs in it. It offers pay-out options on a monthly, quarterly, and half-yearly basis. The investment is for ten years. At the end of 10 years, you get back the purchase price. If anything, unfortunate happens before 10 years, the purchase price is given to the nominee. The interest paid by the scheme is fully taxed as per your applicable slab. There are no tax benefits or deductions available with this scheme. This can be taken by LIC in online or offline mode. It can be a good option for senior citizens to do investments.

Annuity

An annuity is the monthly or annually guaranteed income opted for, after paying a lump sum amount on an immediate basis or over a period of time. This is done with the intention of securing income, post-retirement. An annuity is a contract between you and an insurance company that requires the insurer to make payments to you, either immediately or in the future. The annuity payment is continued till the person insured is alive or up to a fixed term. After the death of an insured person, the nominee gets the lump sum amount that was paid for the annuity. Premium paid is tax deductible under sec 80C.

Annuity helps in getting guaranteed income for life. It is hassle-free, has no maintenance, and is a frictionless option. It is a safe plan as it is not market-linked. It helps in leaving behind a lump sum amount for the next generation. It has a plan which takes care of the spouse through a joint-life option. If you are nearing retirement, you may have a large savings amount that you may want to invest with some fixed amount to be received each month.

Some annuity plans provide you with the option to invest regularly and receive income at a later age for your retirement. This enables you to invest small amounts, thereby making it easy on your pocket. You should start early investments for a guaranteed income for life, especially during the post-retirement period. Pay-out from an annuity plan is used to cover your day-to-day expenses during retirement and to fulfill post-retirement dreams, such as traveling, starting a venture, pursuing a hobby, and much more.

Systematic withdrawal plan

A systematic withdrawal plan is a plan offered by mutual funds to withdraw an amount from their investments periodically. Here you can utilize the corpus created till now. It can serve as a pension for each month. Here you define a percentage of the amount that you require on a month-on-month basis.

For Example: Raman wanted Rs 25000 every month for his expenses. He invested Rs 50 lakhs in SWP and has defined an SWP of 5% every month. So, every month he will receive

Rs25000 as per his requirement. The amount kept in SWP is also generating a return of 8% for him and he continues this for the next 20 years. So, every month he will get Rs 25000 for his expenses and at the same, his capital will also appreciate. In the next 20 years, he will be withdrawing Rs 60 lakhs against the investment of Rs 50 lakhs and still he will be having a final corpus of 90 lakhs after 20 years.

A systematic withdrawal plan is the best way to keep getting the required amount as a pension and still our capital keeps increasing.

Policies paying retirement income

There are different policies currently in the market offering pensions or an income after retirement. For these plans, you have to invest some amounts from today for the next 10-20 years depending on when you want to start getting income and pension. It also depends on the plan you are opting for. And after the specified time, you start getting the decided amount on a monthly basis. But a major thing to consider is inflation before buying such policies. Inflation is a big miss in these policies. As in these policies, you get the same or similar type of amounts you have invested today. Companies might give you that same amount for a longer duration of just 30-35 years, but that will not be sufficient.

For Example: You might require Rs. 30,000 per month for basic expenses. Considering 7% inflation, this requirement will double to Rs. 60000/month after 10 years and Rs. 1,20,000/ month after 20 years.

Current Requirement	Inflation	Requirement After 10 years	Requirement After 20 Yrs
30000/month	7%	60000	1,20,000

But, in these policies let us say if you invest Rs. 10,000 per month for the next 10 years. After a few years, policy companies start giving Rs. 8000-12000 for the next 25-35 years. However, this is way less than what is required. See the below table for a better understanding.

Investment ->	Rs 10000/month for 10 years	
Amount Received after 10 years ->	Rs 8000- Rs12000 / Month for 25-35 years	
Actual Requirement after 10 years ->	Rs 60000/ Month	Shortfall of 48000-52000 / Month
Actual Requirement after 20 years ->	Rs 120000	Shortfall of 48000-52000 / Month

So, check wisely before going for such policies.

Rahul – "*Bhaiya* words are insufficient for thanking you. You have told me to plan things for retirement and how life should be after retirement. I am really grateful to you. I wish everyone has a friend cum brother like you, who can help them with finances, as this is the most important area to look upon to get all the happiness we wanted for ourselves and our family."

Activities:

1: Find out the current return percentage range of the instruments discussed in this chapter.

2: Check the investments in respective products for EEE benefit (For understanding EEE read EEE in chapter 2 of finance concepts before proceeding).

3: As you are aware of interest rates and EEE benefits, now create a plan for reaching the amount you require on monthly basis towards your expenses.

Summary:

Risk capacity might be low after you are retired, depending on your age to retire.

We have discussed the most used investment instruments that can be considered after retirement.

Checking the minute details before buying anything for pensions or regular income is very important.

Chapter 11: Conclusion

"If all you do is set goals and achieve them then you have learned to be a doer. Happiness isn't at the end of the next goal. It is the journey of aligning your choices to mould your character into the type of person who lives their belief system, then creates a life purpose that reflects that same person."

– Shannon L. Alder

You have the roadmap to plan your early retirement and for being rich too. Even if you are not thinking of early retirement, you might have got a proper plan to work on your retirement goal. Methodologies discussed in this book can give you a foundation for other financial goals as well. Francis Bacon quoted, "Knowledge is power". Yes, knowledge gives you the power to understand what is right and what is wrong, and how to behave in certain circumstances, which may be based on learning from other people's experiences or yours. But I will say, that implementing this knowledge into actions is the biggest power. Only gaining knowledge here and there can make you one of the world's most knowledgeable people, but you would be shattered when the bank account is looked upon. We are striving hard day and night to make this world a better place for our family and ourselves. But being extreme in any department, be it savings or enjoying can hurt us badly in the later stages of life. If you have only saved without enjoying your life, you might feel disastrous in the future thinking you have not enjoyed your youth. If you have only enjoyed your youthful days, you might feel disastrous too as then you will not have the proper amount to manage the necessities of life. Hence proper balance is required in life to feel contended in the future.

"Financial life has extreme ends of investment and enjoyment, inclination towards either side makes your future life hell."

"Dreamers think about a dream life, Doers create a dream life."

Whoever you are, young or old, working or homemaker, in a job or in business, employed or unemployed, married or unmarried, male or female, whatever situation you might be in today, just take charge of your life, take action on whatever you have understood from this book, and start your journey towards a better life. Fear of failure is the biggest failure in someone's life as it stops you from taking action or makes you always be in procrastination mode. You might think if I fail what will happen? Any which ways if you are not planning your life, you are planning for a substandard life or a life of misery and I can definitely tell you, if you start taking action then definitely your life will be better than what it would have been if left unplanned. You might think that I am already very late. You might have heard a quote "It's better late than never". Start working on your goals and put the things into action and your life might change as this is the difference between doers and knowledge takers.

"You must gain control over your money or the lack of it will forever control you."

-- Dave Ramsey

Saving and investing is a habit, more sooner it's realized and inculcated, the better your life will be. Financial education is the rarest commodity. Your financial life is no less than a road fighter video game we used to play in childhood. In the game you need to drive a car. The goal is to reach the finish line in different stages without running out of time and hitting other cars. Similarly, imagine your financial life as a road fighter game where you are having different financial goals and the goal here is to finish all the financial goals and reach the finish line of retirement.

Just like the road fighter game, here also time to reach any of the financial goals is limited as you have a defined timeline for child graduation, child marriage , retirement planning and other goals.

In a road fighter game, you avoid hitting other cars. Here you need to avoid financial mistakes as financial mistakes might cause a big downslide making you start your financial journey again from start. Financial mistakes may be investing in many quick rich schemes, buying stocks just because someone told you so and various other financial mistakes that you would have done. In-game you might get various chances to restart and play it again. But in life, finances play a very important role. Financial mistakes can destroy the hardships of investments done till now. So, taking all the steps wisely is very important. You go to a doctor when you fall ill. You go to school and college when you require formal education.

Similarly, when you are stuck in finances or want a specialised solution on loans/ investments/ insurance/ optimizing finances you should not hesitate to go to a finance doctor as he can be a specialist who will solve your queries in a few minutes just like experts in different other fields. From my experience I can tell you clearly, small changes in anyone's financial plan can create big changes for a better future for themselves and their families.

If you want to get your money multifold by :

1) Getting your current inflow of money managed.

2) Learning money management to be self confident and independent.

You can reach out to us on prosperwithrohit@gmail.com

If you still have problems doing or taking action – you can connect with us on

Facebook Page –
https://www.facebook.com/ProsperWithRohit

Facebook Group –
https://www.facebook.com/groups/wealthsecretsbyrohit

Instagram:
https://www.instagram.com/prosperwithrohit/

Linkedin:
https://www.linkedin.com/in/prosperwithrohit

Website: www.prosperwithrohit.com

YouTube: https://prosperwithrohit.click/Youtube

Spotify:

https://spotifyanchor-web.app.link/e/IPZJszmx0wb

Email: prosperwithrohit@gmail.com

Epilogue

The prelude of the book reproduced a picture of the truth that exists in India with a roving truth that exists in urban India. There has been a myriad of irreversible financial crises amongst the once-upon-a-time well-to-do families. I believe that all this can be avoided. Awareness of proper financial insulation should be spread far and wide and we can start with ourselves.

A financial plan serves as a guide as you travel through life. It essentially assists you in gaining control of your income, expenses, and investments, allowing you to manage your money and reach your goals. It gives meaning to your ambitions or dreams. Financial planning enables you to better understand your goals, including why you need to reach them and how they affect other elements of your life and finances. Planning advises you to keep an eye on inflation. A financial plan serves as a guide as you travel through life. Essentially, it allows you to be in. Assistance with financial planning. It also includes considerations for the end of life and beyond. An estate plan developed as part of your overall financial strategy will assist you in ensuring that dependent children are cared for using the assets you have acquired.

"Millions wish for financial freedom, but only those that make it a priority have millions."

Oscar Auliq-Ice

www.ingramcontent.com/pod-product-compliance
Lightning Source LLC
LaVergne TN
LVHW041059150826
845673LV00007B/1836